PEACE IN THE BALKANS

The Movement Towards International Organization in the Balkans

BY

NORMAN J. PADELFORD, Ph.D.

PROFESSOR OF GOVERNMENT
COLGATE UNIVERSITY

NEW YORK

OXFORD UNIVERSITY PRESS

1935

TO MY

MOTHER AND FATHER

PREFACE

To write of peace at a moment when war appears imminent may seem a futile undertaking. And to contemplate peace in South-Eastern Europe, nine times the theatre of war in the past century, must seem an absurdity. Yet there are developments which may lighten dark hopes. The formation of regional groupings, based upon geographical propinquity and common objectives, has been one of the salient features of international relations since the World War. These associations are effective agencies by which the smaller states may make their influence felt and also are useful nuclei for the advancement of co-operation and unity which may lead to peace.

The Balkans have to-day become the seat of one of these movements. The first all-Balkan Conference assembled in Athens in 1930. Since then three other conferences have been held, a permanent organization established, numerous occupational associations founded, and the creation of a 'Balkan conscience' undertaken. The outstanding social, economic, intellectual, as well as political, problems separating the peoples have been examined with a view to the eventual creation of a genuine union. In 1934 the governments officially identified themselves with the endeavour through the formation of the Balkan Entente.

By virtue of its technique of work, the progress which has been made, the strength of the sentiment revealed in favour of union, and in view of its potential influence, the movement for international organization in the Balkans traced in the following pages is one of the most significant developments in international relations. It is a hopeful antidote for the divisive spirit which has been creeping into other realms of international activities. Throughout this study an effort has been made to relate the Balkan plan to the larger trends in European affairs and to the fundamental principles and structure of a permanent organization of world peace.

It sometimes occurs that order emerges from chaos in one place while confusion appears in the most ordered parts. Few anticipated in 1775 the durable union, power, and influence which would result from the co-operative endeavour of the thirteen American colonies. A comparable history for the Balkans, or for a European federation which may grow out of the several regional groupings now in existence, is not immediately to be envisaged. But, at least something more than a mere pantomime of peace is being enacted in the Balkans. Separatism and war may again intervene. Care must be exercised lest the association become merely an amplifier by which to broadcast grievances or a device for the perpetuation of unsatisfactory arrangements. Nevertheless, a movement has been set on foot which, if persevered in, may yet turn the witches' cauldron into the prophets' oracle.

N. J. P.

Hamilton, New York
18 September 1935

CONTENTS

CHAPTER ONE

THE BIRTH OF A BALKAN IDEAL

I

SYNONYMOUS for centuries with intrigue, strife, and the disruption of European peace, the Balkans have today become the seat of a significant movement in international organization, which has as its goal the insurance of peace, the restriction of foreign influence, and the evolution of a federation of all of the Balkan states for the improvement of the political, social, economic, and intellectual life of the peninsula.

The idea of a Balkan federation is not new. At the beginning of the nineteenth century it was proposed by the Serbs as a means of raising the Turkish yoke. In 1821 Greek revolutionaries adopted the idea,[1] while similar proposals designed to accomplish the same end were advanced subsequently in Bulgaria and Rumania.[2] A parliamentary union of all subject nationalities was urged in 1908 but without success.[3] The Austrians proposed in 1910 that a Danubian United States be created, whereby the Balkan states, minus Turkey, would become attached to the Dual Monarchy. To offset this Germanic move, Serbian diplomats with French support endeavoured to build up a genuine Balkan federation, with Turkey included.

---

[1] A. P. Papanastassiou, *Vers L'Union Balkanique,* Paris, 1934, p. 57.

[2] D. Michev and B. Petkov, *La Fédération Balkanique, origine, développement, et perspectives actuelles,* Sofia, 1930, p. 18.

[3] Papanastassiou, *op. cit.,* p. 57.

None of these schemes passed beyond the realm of academic discussion until the Ottoman Empire began to disintegrate. The first practical step was the founding of a private organization at Constantinople for the conciliation of the Balkan nationalities just before the first Balkan war. This received the support of the Young Turks, and had advanced to the stage of a proposal for a new Assembly of Nationalities when the first Balkan war put an end to pacific movements. Intrigue, despotism, foreign pressure, and popular hatreds wrecked the principle of co-operation within the peninsula, and led to the war.

While the military co-operation of Bulgaria, Greece, Montenegro, and Serbia might be regarded as having laid a foundation for subsequent federation, the peace settlement, the speedy development of the second war ranging Greece, Rumania, and Serbia against Bulgaria, and then the World War again dividing the peninsula against itself, revealed how remote was the realization of such an idea. The Balkan states had two fundamental principles to learn : that international organization, to have a lasting character, must be designed to handle the problems of peace as well as of war ; and that the aspirations for national self-determination must be respected by the Balkan states themselves as well as by the Great Powers. The dismemberment of Macedonia, and the predatory attitudes adopted toward Albania, Bulgaria, and Turkey made permanent peace as impossible as did the rape of Bosnia and Herzegovina by Austria-Hungary in 1908.

The ravages of the World War were so incisive upon the mind and emotions, that the creation of an equitable international organization embracing all the Balkan states was as impossible in the Balkans in 1919 as in western Europe. Nations thought only of fortifying themselves against a renewal of hostilities, of establishing improved territorial positions for such an eventuality, and of coping with the titanic internal economic and social problems created by the war. But if the creation of such an organization was unthinkable, minds were not lacking to suggest partial organizations, which might or might not become general depending upon the course of events. At the Congress of Oppressed Nationalities held at Rome on the 10th-12th April, 1918, the way was paved for future collaboration among the Czechs, the Yugoslavs, the Poles, and the Rumanians, when representatives of these groups undertook to examine together the coming problems of peace-making.[4] While the Congress emphasized the right of each of these oppressed nationalities to constitute its own nationality and state unity, it did not pledge the parties to any agreement that in the peace settlement the principle which they sought for themselves should be applied with equal and conscientious force for the defeated nationalities, as indeed, the treaties demonstrated.

The Rome meeting was followed in the autumn of 1918 by a series of negotiations between Benes of Czechoslovakia, Venizelos of Greece, Jonescu of Rumania, and Pashitch of Serbia.[5] The conversations were largely due to the energy and foresight of Dr. Benes, Foreign Minister of the newly recognized Czechoslovakia, who saw that unless the small countries were united when the peace was made, their wishes would not receive adequate attention, and they might

[4] Machray, R., *The Little Entente*, New York, 1930, pp. 73-75.
[5] *Ibid.*, pp. 85-86.

easily be sacrificed to the political considerations of the Great Powers. The discussions revolved about two different axes : the Hapsburg domains, and the Balkans. Two schemes of organization emerged from these discussions. The first one, championed by Benes, sought to unite the Czechs, Rumanians, and Yugoslavs in an association to offset dangers arising from Austria and Hungary. This plan opened the way for the Little Entente conventions between these three states in 1920-1921.[6]

The second plan, advocated by Take Jonescu who was then Prime Minister of Rumania, differed from the first one only in the size and membership of the association. Jonescu wanted an entente which would include Greece and Poland also, and thus form a cordon stretching from the Ægean to the Baltic.[7] While Premier Jonescu's general plan failed of acceptance in 1918, the ideas which he set forth in connection with it, nevertheless, may be found embodied almost without change in both the Little Entente, and now the Balkan Entente. Writing in the *Revue de France* in November 1921, Jonescu said that Benes, Pashitch, Venizelos, and he had agreed that there should be "a treaty of alliance between the five states guaranteeing to each other the integrity of our frontiers, a permanent contact should be established between the five Ministers of Foreign Affairs so that our action in international affairs shall be in common, one seat occupied in turn by each of us should be de-

---

[6] See Machray, *op. cit.*, Chapters III and IV; Crane, J. O., *The Little Entente*, New York, 1931, Chapter I ; Codrescu, F., *La Petite Entente*, Paris, 1933, Vol. I, Sec. 3, Chapter I. The texts of the three agreements are reproduced in the Appendix to facilitate comparison with the Balkan Pact of Entente.

[7] Machray, *op. cit.*, p. 86; Crane, *supra*, p. 7.

manded on the permanent Committee of the League of Nations ... finally, military instruction and armaments should be organized on the same plan in the five countries." [8]

Both the Benes plan, which brought into existence the Little Entente in 1920-1921, and the Jonescu plan, which has not yet found embodiment in a single treaty, contributed much to that "ferment of ideas" which eventually led to the movement for international organization in the Balkans. Both plans, but more especially the Little Entente, were instrumental in obtaining recognition for the principle of regional security pacts, which, though never legalized by amendment of the Covenant of the League of Nations,[9] have come to be the accepted order of the day.

The formal hostilities of the World War itself were no sooner ended than informal ones developed between Bulgaria and Yugoslavia over Macedonia, and formal ones flamed up anew between Greece and Turkey. Good relations existed between Rumania, Yugoslavia, and Greece in 1922 as a result of the Little Entente convention, royal inter-marriages, and common victory at the expense of Bulgaria. These, together with memories of the association in the Balkan wars, formed an adequate basis for commonalty of approach to the Balkan problems and may be said to mark a foundation for organization. As the Græco-Turk fighting drew to a close and the Lausanne Conference approached with its possibility of a general consideration of the Balkan and Near Eastern questions, these three states ex-

[8] Take Jonescu, "La Petite Entente," *Revue de France*, Paris, 1 November, 1929, p. 17.

[9] Benes sought such an amendment in 1921. Machray, *op. cit.*, pp. 155-156.

changed notes quite naturally and agreed upon the presentation of a common front.[10] Bulgaria, plunged into economic chaos as a result of the war, and generally disaffected by the losses sustained in the Dobrudja, Macedonia, and Thrace, and by the failure of Greece to accord her the outlet to the Ægean provided for in Article 48 of the Treaty of Neuilly, made a serious effort to associate herself with this grouping. Stambulisky, the peasant Prime Minister, visited Bucharest and Belgrade in an effort to resolve the disputes and rescue his country from isolation. At Belgrade he proposed that the Macedonian situation be handled by the appointment of a mixed commission to meet on the spot, investigate all situations and incidents, and propose an acceptable solution to the two countries.[11] This met with Yugoslavian acceptance but came to naught in subsequent years as a result of the machinations of the terroristic Internal Macedonian Revolutionary Organization of Bulgaria. In 1932 it was again recurred to by the Balkan Conference, as will be seen later, as part of a plan of achieving Balkan organization. In return for the Bulgarian initiative, Yugoslavia agreed to support Bulgarian claims for the Ægean outlet, and actually did so at the Lausanne Conference, but without success for she at the same time insisted that there should be absolutely no modification of the terms of the Treaty of Neuilly.[12]

At the time of the Lausanne Conference in 1922, then, there was a semblance of unity and reconciliation

[10] Machray, *op. cit.*, p. 208.
[11] *Ibid.*, p. 208.
[12] Machray, *op. cit.*, p. 208.

among four of the Balkan states. To be sure, it was a victors' friendship among three of them, likely to suffer all of the customary consequences thereof. But the Bulgarian association with these three must be described as otherwise, and the unity of the four, even though temporary, was a hopeful augury for the future, and may be said to mark the second tangible evidence of the gathering of forces favourable to the eventual creation of Balkan organization. To be sure, Turkey was at that moment generally despised and regarded with suspicion, and the Albanians isolated in their mountain fastness commonly overlooked or held in contempt.

Balkan relations soon lapsed back into a parlous condition. Assassinations and terroristic acts within Bulgaria and Yugoslavia poisoned their accord. Resentment and mutual recrimination characterized Græco-Turk relations following Lausanne. Græco-Bulgarian relations were so bad in 1925 that only forceful action by the League of Nations Council forestalled actual war.[13] Rumania's attention was fastened upon Hungarian and Soviet developments. All semblance of collaboration save between Czechoslovakia, Rumania, and Yugoslavia vanished. Albania, Bulgaria, Greece, and Turkey were not only isolated from the other states, but were at swords-points with each other.

Under these circumstances the suggestion, made after the conclusion of the Locarno pacts, that a Balkan "Locarno" be drawn up met with little success. While the proposition was canvassed in the various capitals and

[13] Sir Eric Drummond, *Ten Years of World Co-operation*, Geneva, 1930, pp. 31-37 ; Morley, *The Society of Nations*, Washington, 1932, pp. 467-469 ; *Official Journal*, League of Nations, November 1925, p. 1696 *et seq.*

by the ministers of the Little Entente,[14] it was hope-
lessly impossible in such an atmosphere of atrocities and
mass deportations. The representatives of the Little
Entente publicly announced their acceptance of the plan
in principle, but the proposal was shelved following
definite indications from Yugoslavia that she first desired to remove her difficulties with Bulgaria and Greece,
and from Turkey that she was opposed to the general
idea itself. In view of the subsequent lack of faith in
the Locarno agreements, and the dissipation of the
"Locarno spirit," the Balkan states were undoubtedly
wiser in first settling their disputes, for mere pactology
alone can never ensure peace.

Prospects of Balkan co-operation increased measurably
after 1928. Venizelos, returning to power in Greece,
infused a more liberal attitude into Balkan diplomacy.
Immediate steps were taken by Greece to renew relations with all states and to settle outstanding disputes.
In succession, the relations with Italy, Rumania, Bulgaria, Yugoslavia, and Turkey were improved and treaties of amity signed with each. Other states followed
suit, and the Balkans soon became entwined with a host
of bilateral treaties. One of the most important of
these was an agreement between Bulgaria and Yugoslavia which provided for a mixed commission on the
Macedonian problems, the setting up of a neutral zone
running along both sides of the frontier, and the settlement of the contentious issue of double property.[15]
Although the majority of these pacts unfortunately

---

[14] Timisoara Meeting, 10th February, 1926. See R. Machray, *The
Little Entente*, New York, 1930, pp. 276-277 ; J. O. Crane, *The Little
Entente*, New York, 1931, pp. 126-127, 175 ; Codrescu, *La Petite Entente*,
Paris, 1933, Vol. II, pp. 7-11.

[15] Crane, *op. cit.*, pp. 121-122 ; Codrescu, *supra*, Vol. II, pp. 156-157.

appear to have been made with an eye to protection against one another,[16] and although a net-work of bi-lateral treaties is no substitute for organization within one compact, the establishment of understanding and confidence between individual states is, nevertheless, a wise if not fundamental prerequisite to a permanent structure of peace.

II

THE idea of concerted action became evident at the Inter-Parliamentary Conference on Commerce at Berlin in 1929. The Balkan representatives held a common front to the proposals made in the Conference, and favourably backed a suggestion of M. Caphandaris of Greece for a Balkan parliamentary conference in spite of the opposition of representatives of the Great Powers.[17]

The real birth of the movement appropriately took place in Athens at the meeting of the Universal Peace Congress in 1929. In the course of the study of M. Briand's proposal for a European federation, made at the Assembly of the League of Nations in 1928, M. Papanastassiou, former President of the Council of Ministers of Greece, suggested that a semi-official conference be called to consider the possibilities of federation among the Balkan states.[18] The suggestion was eagerly received by the Congress and caused *"une vive sensation."* With the aid of the Bureau International de la Paix at Geneva contact was made with each of the

---

[16] It still seems to be an almost inescapable circumstance of Eastern European affairs that no two countries can make a gesture of friendship or collaboration without arousing the suspicions of all others.

[17] Papanastassiou, *op. cit.*, p. 11.

[18] XXVII Congrès Universel de la Paix, *Documents Officiel*, Geneva, 1929, p. 237.

Balkan governments,[19] which agreed to lend a measure
of support to the proposal.[20]   An agenda was drawn
up, a basis for the selection of delegates determined,
and invitations sent out by the Bureau.[21]

The agenda was carefully drawn so as to avoid giving
offence to any state or the raising of issues which might
immediately plunge the Conference into irreconcilable
controversy.   It called for a discussion of all questions
having a special interest to the Balkan states and of any
steps that might be taken to aid Balkan co-operation.
In particular, the agenda called for the consideration
of :

  I. (a) General principles governing the organization of
           a Balkan Union.
      (b) Organization of the Balkan Conferences.
 II. Measures useful for advancing the political and in-
      tellectual reconciliation of the Balkan countries.
III. Measures for advancing economic co-operation.[22]

In determining the basis of choosing delegations some
difficulty was experienced.   It was first thought that
the Conference should be an inter-parliamentary conference, with delegates chosen as for the larger body.
But it was recognized that the Yugoslavian parliamentary system was not functioning normally, and that
such a conference would not represent all walks of life.[23]
It was decided, therefore, that each country should be
asked to send not less than ten nor more than thirty
delegates and that in selecting them an effort should
be made to present a cross-section of national life and

[19] *Le Mouvement Pacifiste* (Geneva), October-December 1929, p. 123.
[20] *Ibid.*, April-June 1930, p. 32 ; *ibid.*, July-August 1930, p. 52.
[21] *Ibid.*, April-June 1930, pp. 37-41.
[22] *Ibid.*, July-August 1930, p. 53.
[23] Papanastassiou, *op. cit.*, p. 13.

thought.[24]   It was provided that there should be equal voting power, regardless of the size of the delegations. It was further decided that the foreign minister of the country in which the Conference met should be requested to invite the other foreign ministers to meet and to confer at the time and place of the Conference.[25]

In June 1930, prior to the assembling of the Conference in October, the Greek Chamber of Deputies discussed the movement favourably and instructed its president to communicate to the other Balkan legislatures the pleasure with which the Greek government welcomed the Conference.   It also ordered the Director-General of the Ministry of Foreign Affairs to attend as an observer.[26]   This gracious move evoked favourable reactions in the other legislatures, and resulted in the appointment of the ambassadors at Athens as official observers.

The first Conference opened auspiciously at Athens the 5th October, 1930, with representatives from all the Balkan countries. Although Albania and Bulgaria had hesitated to send delegates because of the non-inclusion of the minorities question on the agenda, they were finally won over upon the suggestion that there could be no Balkan union or political agreement without prior satisfactory settlement of that issue.[27]   Ninety-nine delegates attended, many of whom were persons of high standing and political responsibility.[28]   Among the observers were the diplomatic corps at Athens, rep-

---

[24] Papanastassiou, *op. cit.*, p. 13 ; Haberlin, *supra*, p. 3.

[25] *Ibid.*, p. 14.

[26] *Ibid.*, pp. 61-62.

[27] *L'Esprit International*, January 1931, p. 9.

[28] *Le Mouvement Pacifiste*, September-November 1930, p. 81 ; Haberlin, *op. cit.*, p. 4.

resentatives of the League of Nations Secretariat, the International Labour Office, the European Customs Union, the Inter-Parliamentary Conference on Commerce, the International Chamber of Commerce, the Bureau International de la Paix, and the Carnegie Endowment for International Peace.

At the opening session Premier Venizelos gave the movement the support of the Greek government and aptly set the stage for the proceedings, saying, "No one fails to appreciate the difficulty of bringing about a union of the Balkan States ; we all recognize that it can be accomplished only by stages. But if you begin with the points on which agreement is easier, you will create an atmosphere in which the successive settlement of more difficult questions, about which differences of opinion are at present more serious, will become possible." [29] M. Ciceo-Pop, the leading Rumanian delegate, furthered the proceedings not only by hailing the movement, as indeed did all of the delegation spokesmen, and pledging the support of his government, but by pointing out that no Balkan entente was conceivable which did not take as a fundamental principle the loyal execution of treaties, including the minority provisions.[30]

In an atmosphere of conciliation, realism, and good sense a foundation was laid. Commissions were established to deal with questions of : (1) organization ; (2) political relations ; (3) intellectual co-operation ; (4) economic relations ; (5) communications ; (6) social problems. Each country was given the presidency of a commission, and the membership of the Conference divided itself into these groups where the real work was

[29] Toynbee, *Survey of International Affairs,* 1930. London, 1931, p. 155.
[30] Haberlin, *op. cit.,* p. 5.

done. A Bureau was instituted, composed of the chief delegates and delegation secretaries. This Bureau aided the committees in finding solutions for their difficulties,[31] while the Council which was created at the same time handled the business of the Conference proceedings.[32]

The work of the Conference may be said to have divided itself into two parts. The first was the consideration of the broad lines upon which union might be eventually achieved. The second phase of the work involved the examination of practical measures of immediate co-operation which would also serve the ultimate goal. The work of the Conference regarding the first part was directed by M. Papanastassiou of Greece whose exhaustive and prophetic report opened the subject.[33] Peace, freedom from influence and intrigue, and the rational development of the economic life of the peninsula are, according to the report, the objects to be sought by union. In order to attain these ends, political, economic, social, and intellectual union are essential. The form of union must lie in the realm between a free association of nationalities and genuine federation. It must not be so restrictive as the United States of America, yet more powerful than the League of Nations. It must recognize and secure personal and ethnical rights, yet it must not derogate the sovereignty of any state. By systematic collaboration and the harmonization of the forces of good, it must seek the best for all. All must be united by a multi-partite

[31] Papanastassiou, *op. cit.*, p. 64.

[32] *Ibid.*, p. 64.

[33] "Rapport sur les principes essentiels devant servir de base à l'Union Balkanique." *Documents Officiels de la Première Conférence Balkanique,* Athens, 1930.

agreement within the framework of the League of Nations, a possible European federation, and the Kellogg-Briand Pact.[34]

In examining the motives which made the realization of political co-operation possible, the Commission on Political Questions, and the Conference itself, found a most delicate situation. The mere mention of boundaries or minorities threatened to disrupt the entire proceedings. Careful engineering, constant emphasis upon the desirability and need of union, and upon the preparatory and inaugural nature of the Conference, plus a general desire to avoid a breakdown, saved the day for all parties and resulted in the adoption of an elementary but important resolution. Setting forth the unanimous desire of the Balkan peoples for peace, for the resolution of all difficulties, for the reinforcement of existing treaties, including those relative to minorities, the Conference advocated that the foreign ministers meet each year to discuss all questions before their states interfering with the establishment of understanding, that a study be started looking toward the eventual realization of a Balkan pact involving outlawry of war, amicable settlement of all disputes, and mutual assistance, and that the Council appoint such a committee to report at the next Conference.[35]

The Commission on Organization directed its attention to the foundation of a permanent statute for the Conferences. It was confronted with fewer obstacles than the Political Commission, and its labours were

---

[34] See statement by Venizelos, *Le Messager d'Athènes*, 6th January, 1931.

[35] Resolutions, *Documents Officiels de la Première Conférence Balkanique*, Athens, 1930, pp. 1-2 ; *Le Mouvement Pacifiste*, September-November 1930, pp. 82-83 ; Papanastassiou, *op. cit.*, pp. 78-79.

crowned by the adoption of its proposed statute.[36] According to the statute, the Balkan Conference exists to contribute to the federation of the Balkan peoples. The Conference is to meet every year. The organs of the Conference are the General Assembly, Council, Bureau, and National Groups. The latter are the members of past and present delegations. Their duty is to associate all peace and political groups behind the movement, to keep public opinion in their country in touch with opinion in the other countries, to help select delegations for future conferences, and to work for the application of the Conference resolutions in their country. They are required to submit an annual report of their activities. Each country is entitled to thirty delegates, plus experts, secretaries, and observers. If less than thirty attend, plural voting will be permitted so that each group shall have the equivalent of thirty votes. On the commissions each country is to have at least two representatives but not more than five votes. The Conference has a President and five Vice-Presidents. The President of the Conference becomes the President of the Council until January 31st when the office passes to the head of another national group. The Council is the executive body of the Conference, meeting between sessions, fixing the agenda, approving the budget, and taking any action deemed necessary. It is composed of the chiefs and two other members of each national group. It may be summoned by the President on the demand of seven members. The secretariat is headed by a Secretary-General. The finances are cared for by annual pro-rata contributions, determined each year by the Council. Finally, the statute authorizes a Balkan

[36] Resolutions, *supra*, pp. 3-4 ; Papanastassiou, *op. cit.*, pp. 86-88.

flag, as if to proclaim to the world the existence of a new political entity.

The mechanical structure provided for by the statute differs little from that found in other international organizations. Perhaps its sole claim to uniqueness lies in its studied effort to reach and to co-ordinate all phases of Balkan life, public and private. Too often private international organization appeals to one group or interest with little consideration for the other phases of life, and too often public international organization is subject to the whims and pressures of narrow political strategy, as may be seen in the disarmament or economic conferences. While the League of Nations has at times sought to steer clear of these reefs, no organization which is exclusively private or public can avoid them entirely. In combining representatives of government, employers, and employees, the International Labour Organization has successfully maintained a broad and comprehensive policy toward the problems of labour. The weakness inherent in an international organization combining public and private representatives lies, of course, in the possibility of evading responsibility. If the Balkan group can successfully unite the private and the public forces — the 1934 Pact shows that it has not been done yet — it will perform a notable service to the cause of constructive international organization.

The Commission on Economic Affairs examined at length the economic situation in each country and in the region in general. Inter-Balkan trade was confronted everywhere with high, discriminatory tariffs ; each country was blindly following mercantilist doctrine by trying to sell to its neighbours without buying in return and by endeavouring to make itself economically

self-sufficient ; each was primarily an agricultural community raising the same commodities as its neighbours ;
each was confronted with the gradual loss of its foreign
markets owing to the economic crisis and to cut-throat
competition ; each was threatened with a credit crisis
from over-borrowing ; each was subordinating economic
welfare to military policies. In an area of 1,200,000
square kilometers and 60,000,000 population, inter-
Balkan commerce was found to amount to only 9% of
the total foreign commerce of the states.[37]

While economic union might seem a hopeless dream,
it was realized, nevertheless, that there could be no
political union without economic union also. It was
further seen that economic union would mean greater
bargaining power in foreign markets, greater protection
for Balkan crops, an opportunity to engage in specializa-
tion, and better use of the soil.[38] With these things in
mind, the Economics Commission submitted to the
Conference a series of proposals requesting: (1) consideration of a plan for a customs and monetary union involving the lowering of tariff barriers, and the setting-up
of an inter-Balkan bank ; (2) promotion of economic
collaboration and protection of common Balkan products
with "most favoured nation" treatment for each other's
goods ; (3) unification of tariff nomenclatures ; (4)
establishment of offices in each country for the promotion of commerce ; (5) co-operation of credit agencies ;
(6) common action for the protection and furtherance
of the oriental tobacco trade.[39] These measures were
adopted by the Conference, together with a request that

[37] Papanastassiou, *op. cit.*, p. 37 ; D. Michev and B. Petkov, *supra*, p. 31.
[38] *Ibid.*, pp. 39-40.
[39] Resolutions, *supra*, pp. 3-4 ; *Le Mouvement Pacifiste*, September-November 1930, p. 83.

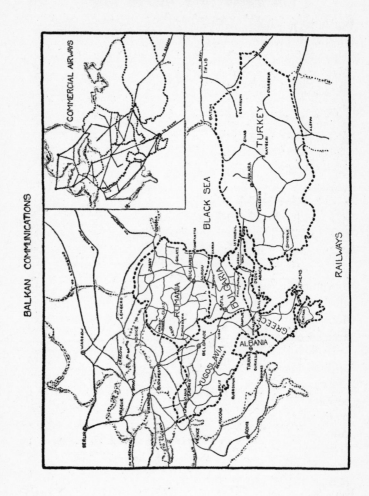

the Balkan governments should take steps for the conclusion of a pact of economic solidarity.

In examining the situation respecting railway, maritime, air, highway, telegraphic and telephonic communications, the Communications Commission found a hopeless muddle. Judged by even moderate standards of efficiency and economic welfare, there was a general deficiency in this field. Direct connections were lacking between most capitals. In order to go from Bucharest to Athens it was necessary to go either by water round the Hellespont, or via Belgrade if by rail. Albania was inaccessible by rail or by highway from any Balkan state. There was not a bridge across the Danube in the Balkan area. Long-distance telephones were lacking between many cities. Railroads and highways frequently ran only to frontiers without being continued across into neighbouring states. Train schedules were made practically without thought for connections in other states, and railway fares were frequently discriminatory.

Numerous suggestions were made for the gradual improvement of the situation. These included the construction of direct rail, air, road, and telegraphic lines between all the capitals ; the construction of two main trunk lines (rail and road) through the Balkans, one to run from the Black Sea to the Adriatic, and the other from the Danube to the Ægean Sea. Sufficient measure of agreement was found upon postal questions to permit the drafting and adoption of an Inter-Balkan Postal Convention to go into effect in April 1931. This was modeled after and made an affiliated part of the Universal Postal Union.[40]

[40] Resolutions, *supra*, pp. 4-6.

The Committee on Intellectual Co-operation began its labours with the hypothesis that any form of federation or union must be preceded and constantly accompanied by intellectual and moral amity, sincerity, and understanding.[41] In the resolution adopted by the Conference it was noted that there was an absence of such understanding and that the prevailing intellectual isolation fostered misunderstanding, prejudices, and hatreds. To remedy the situation it was suggested that there be exchanges of students and professors, the creation of libraries and professorships to emphasize Balkanism, athletic and scholastic competitions, changes in the teaching and writing of Balkan history, and translations of Balkan folklore. The resolution also recommended the elimination of travel barriers, and the inauguration of Balkan Weeks in each country.[42]

The Commission on Social Policies covered a good deal of ground in its examination of social conditions and social legislation in the various countries. In the resolutions which were adopted by the Conference, attention was called to measures needed to ameliorate the conditions of labourers, the principles which should underlie social legislation, the desirability of concluding labour conventions, the promotion of co-operation between professional groups, the urgency of fair treatment for foreign workers, the need for better hygienic services and the suppression of prostitution.[43]

In addition to the resolutions coming from these various committees, the plenary session of the Con-

---

[41] Papanastassiou, *op. cit.*, p. 42.

[42] Resolutions, *supra*, pp. 2-3.

[43] *Ibid.*, pp. 6-7 ; *Le Mouvement Pacifiste*, September-November 1930, p. 83 ; *Survey of International Affairs*, 1930, pp. 155-156.

ference requested the study of the unification of Balkan law, and the conclusion of a Balkan extradition treaty.[44]

III

THIS Conference was indeed historic. For the first time a Balkan group gathered without the shadow and the psychology of war above it. For the first time an attempt was made to think through and plan for a constructive era of peace in which the common development of all should take precedence over the exclusive development of any one state or group of states. The Conference demonstrated that although the issues separating the states are deep and serious, they are not incompatible with ultimate union, provided they are attacked in the right spirit and with a lofty ideal. It further showed that there were powerful forces for peace and collaboration at hand — more than had been realized theretofore — and, that when united, tremendous steps were possible within a relatively brief time. The work of the Commissions revealed the real backwardness of the Balkans. The number, catholicity, and constructiveness of the proposals not only pointed the way to the advantages and possibilities of pacific rather than violent measures of solution, but also showed the people what constructive statesmanship might and should accomplish. A beginning was made in the creation of a "Balkan conscience." Finally, the Conference brought into existence a permanent organization, albeit only semi-public, to serve the ideal of union.

The Conference was accompanied by a series of fêtes, games, and receptions. A visit was made to Delphos, seat of the ancient Amphyctionic Council, and a session

[44] *Ibid.*, p. 2.

was held on the Acropolis. The Conference evoked praise from the Balkan press which took active steps after its sessions for the formation of a Balkan press association. Finally, the Greek Government graciously bestowed high decorations upon the various leading delegates from the different countries.[45]

[45] *Le Messager d'Athènes*, 13th January, 1931.

CHAPTER TWO

IDEALISM AND REALITY

I

THE statute of organization of the Balkan Conferences provided for the assembling of the Council mid-way between the meetings of the Conference.

The first meeting of the Council took place in Salonika, January 30-February 2, 1931. At this meeting the leaders of the Pan-Balkan movement canvassed the general Balkan scene, reviewed the work and results of the first Conference, and endeavoured to set the stage for the next gathering. Relative calm was observed to be pervading the Balkans, save for the intermittent flare-up of party politics in Greece and Rumania. The dictatorships in Turkey and Yugoslavia were busy consolidating their work and providing material improvements for their nations. Between Bulgaria and Yugoslavia a new spirit seemed to be emerging as frontier and land issues were put on the road to settlement. Economic life alone showed the signs of danger. Stability was giving way to instability ; public works were being curtailed ; loans were difficult to obtain ; markets shrank and the prices for Balkan goods dropped alarmingly. Far from being discouraged, the Conference leaders saw in the times unusual opportunities for their co-operative work.

In reviewing the work of the past Conference, how-

ever, the Council was forced to recognize that up to the
time of meeting no steps had been taken to apply any of
the resolutions and that little attention had been paid to
the movement subsequent to the adjournment.[1] Little
difficulty was experienced in drafting the agenda for
the next Conference. After agreement that consideration of the projected Balkan pact should form the first
item on the agenda, dissension arose. The Albanians
and Bulgarians, not desirous of seeing themselves out-
manœuvered on the issue of minorities, insisted that a
consideration of this be placed second on the agenda,
and maintained that they could not consider the acceptance of any pact until that issue had been satisfactorily
settled.[2] The Yugoslavians asserted that the minorities
question was outside the competence of the Balkan Conference and belonged only to the League of Nations.
The conflict in the Council was resolved by a Greek
suggestion that inasmuch as the minorities issue was
apparently so closely linked with the question of a pact
it might be most profitably examined by the same committee which was to consider the pact. However, while
this idea was accepted by the Council, communications
from Sofia indicated that all would not be smooth sailing
at the coming Conference.[3]

[1] *Le Messager d'Athènes*, 14th January, 1931.

[2] Papanastassiou, *op. cit.*, p. 96. The Bulgarian attitude is well presented by Professor Georges P. Guenor in an article entitled "La Bulgarie
et les Conférences Balkaniques" in the *Revue Bulgare* (Sofia, 1931). If
the parties, so runs the argument, do not resolve their differences before
they make a union, the issues will inevitably rise to threaten the agreements and the break will be a more serious affair than the present
unsettled condition. There are five million Bulgarians in Bulgaria and
over two million in neighbouring states. There cannot be any *rapprochement* until these minorities are accorded all of the rights guaranteed to
them by the peace treaties. Bulgarian opinion cannot tolerate the idea of
union until its co-nationals are justly treated.

[3] *Survey of International Affairs*, 1931, p. 332.

The Council, in addition to specifying a continuation of the studies begun in the six committees of the first Conference, added to the agenda the discussion of projects involving an Institute of Historical Research, a Balkan Chamber of Commerce, the status of married women, and disarmament. The Council session was closed with the fortuitous receipt and acceptance of an offer of $10,000 from the Carnegie Endowment for International Peace for the support of the Conference Secretariat.[4]

In the winter and spring, "Balkan Weeks" were held in the various capitals, during which there were conferences of special groups, lectures, exhibitions, and contests. Conferences of sport and travel associations were held at Istanbul ; of bankers and industrialists at Salonika and Athens respectively ; of feminist groups at Belgrade ; of agriculturalists and press associations at Sofia ; of municipal representatives at Tirana ; and of intellectual leaders at Belgrade.[5] As was remarked by Professor Toynbee, "The successful organization of the 'Balkan Week' was a proof that the movement for co-operation was not lacking in vitality."[6]

II

BETWEEN the meetings of the Balkan Conferences, the movement for Balkan Union operated in competition with numerous other currents seeking to enlist the support of part of the states to the exclusion of others. Whereas the Balkan movement sought to build an economic and political solidarity among all of the

[4] *Le Mouvement Pacifiste*, January-February 1931, p. 17.
[5] *Les Balkans*, Athens, December-January 1932, p. 214 ; Papanastassiou, *op. cit.*, p. 99.
[6] *Survey of International Affairs*, 1931, p. 334.

Balkan countries, other movements sought to detach certain states for affiliation with groupings of an extra-Balkan character. The Little Entente, in order to consolidate its political power, began consideration of measures of economic unification, which might eventually embarrass Balkan efforts. Developments in the direction of agrarian co-operation among the East European states also overlapped the movement. Conferences looking toward the co-ordination of production, distribution, and marketing were held successively in Warsaw (August 1930), Bucharest (October 1930), Belgrade (November 1930), and subsequently again in Bucharest and Belgrade in the spring of 1931.[7] At these conferences Bulgarians, Rumanians, and Yugoslavians met with representatives from the Central and Baltic states. Wheat conferences were also held at Rome and at London in the spring of 1931, at which only part of the Balkan states were represented. At all of these meetings, as well as at the meetings of the League of Nations Committee of Inquiry for a European Union, from which Turkey was excluded, and at the Central European Economic Council at Vienna in March 1931, the orientation was definitely away from the Balkans.

However, with respect to each of these other movements there are factors which sooner or later are likely to lead to their demise in favour of a Balkan union. The Little Entente does not form an economic unity and its community of interest is restricted largely to the preservation of the treaty *status quo,* which economic, social, and political interest may eventually wish changed.

[7] Crane, *The Little Entente,* pp. 157-160 ; *Current History Magazine,* New York, October 1930, p. 141 ; *Ibid.,* December 1930, p. 460.

The agrarian movement deals with only one phase of the economic crisis, and makes no provision for the alleviation of those social and political problems which divide Central and Eastern Europe. It furthermore omits Soviet Russia, the major agrarian unit of Europe. But above all, each of these competing movements still leaves the door open to foreign intrigue and manipulation, a danger which Balkan history has shown to be only too real and disastrous. Finally, neither of these other movements is likely to give the Balkan peoples the prestige and the influence in international affairs which consolidation within the peninsula would convey.

If external affairs exerted a centripetal influence on some of the Balkan states in 1931, events were not wanting to produce a centrifugal effect. Græco-Turkish *rapprochement,* first manifest by the Ankara Pact of Amity in 1930, resulted during the year in the conclusion of agreements for arbitration, equality of armaments, visits of expatriates, suppression of smuggling, and common protection of the tobacco trade.[8] While it could scarcely be contended that the reconciliation of two states alone would turn the tide in favour of union ; nevertheless, in a region as torn with past animosities as the Balkans, the establishment of warm agreement between any two of the states is a factor hardly to be disregarded. Furthermore, the consolidation and co-operation of any two involves the elimination of a certain amount of manipulation by the Great Powers, and permits the two collaborating states to gain increased influence among their neighbours, with the result that the others are forced to turn greater attention inward to the region and to seek a system of collab-

[8] *Survey of International Affairs,* 1931, pp. 326-328.

oration which will give their voice equal weight, a system which must eventually find its form in organization and union.

The second Balkan Conference met at Istanbul the 20th October, 1931, under favourable conditions. A larger number of delegates, experts, and observers were in attendance,[9] and the Conference received hearty support from the Turkish government. The Conference was opened with a salutatory address by the Turkish Premier, Ismet Pasha. He said that the presence of so many delegates was evidence of the sincerity of the movement, but added that to be successful it must rest upon equality and full recognition of the rights of all people.[10]

The address of the Premier was followed by speeches from each of the delegation leaders, reporting upon the work of their national groups and the status of the movement in their countries. Mehmet Bey Konitza, president of the Albanian group, reported the Albanian people overwhelmingly in favour of a Balkan entente, although he admitted that the Albanian group itself had done little for the movement in the past year.[11] Dr. Sakazoff, head of the Bulgarian group, emphasized the will of his people to live in peace with all neighbours. While saying that legitimate grievances and unjust wrongs could not be disregarded, he added the conciliatory note that all must combat the remembrances of past hatreds and work within their own countries

---

[9] Papanastassiou, *op. cit.*, pp. 100-101 ; Carnegie Endowment for International Peace, *Annual Report of the Director of the Division of Intercourse and Education*, 1931, New York, 1931, p. 64.

[10] Mimeographed Bulletin, Address of Ismet Pasha, 20th October, 1931, *Agence Anatolie.*

[11] Mimeographed Bulletin, Discourse of President of Albanian delegation, *Agence Anatolie*, Istanbul, 1931.

against prejudices and ill-feelings.[12] M. Papanastassiou reported that all resolutions of the first Conference had been submitted to the Greek Parliament ;
that the Greek government had accepted the Balkan
Postal Union ; and that an active propaganda in favour
of the movement was being carried on by the national
group.[13] Hassan Bey, leader of the Turkish group and
President of the Council, said that the movement was
one of long duration and no one should be discouraged
with the slowness of material progress in any one year.[14]
The Yugoslavian leader urged action in the economic
realm without waiting for political union, and suggested
the advisability of concluding non-aggression and conciliation treaties as a prerequisite to union.[15]

The agenda for this Conference contained eight items
which dovetailed into a continued study of the matters
under consideration at the first Conference. The
agenda included : (1) drafting of a Balkan pact of
union ; (2) loyal application of existing treaties, including those applying to minorities, and examination of
all questions hindering political co-operation of the peoples ; (3) common protection for cereals and tobacco ;
(4) collaboration of banking institutions ; (5) freedom
of circulation and of work for aliens ; (6) collaboration
of sanitary services ; (7) railway agreement and construction of necessary bridges ; (8) unification of civil
law.[16]

The sub-committee on the pact of union submitted its
report to the Political Commission. The pact and

---

[12] Mimeographed Bulletin, *Ibid.*
[13] *Ibid.*
[14] *Ibid.*
[15] *Ibid.*
[16] *Le Mouvement Pacifiste*, September-October 1931, p. 95.

treaty-enforcement issues became the major bones of contention in the Commission and in the Conference proper. The proposed pact, drafted by Professor Spiropoulos, and patterned after the Little Entente's General Act of Conciliation, Arbitration, and Judicial Settlement,[16a] involved an agreement of non-aggression, pacific solution of differences by a Balkan Conciliation Commission or the World Court, and mutual assistance against any Balkan state making an aggression upon any other Balkan state.[17] While not quarreling with the principles of the project, the Bulgarian delegation, supported by the Albanians, immediately suggested an adjournment of the discussion on the projected pact until a solution had been found for the issues arising out of the non-fulfillment of minorities treaties. Such acrimonious debate ensued that little progress was made. The Commission was saved from a deadlock by the suggestion that the Conference seek to discover the best ways of fulfilling treaties, and by the Albanian suggestion, later incorporated in the pact, that commissions be set up in each state to preside over the enforcement of treaties.[18]

Just prior to the close of the Conference a sufficient measure of agreement was obtained upon four resolutions to obtain their passage. The first resolution reveals how inextricably united had become the questions of pacts and of minorities.

"The Conference : Being of the opinion that, in order to prepare the ground for the closest co-operation between

---

[16a] See Appendix II.

[17] Papanastassiou, *op. cit.*, p. 102. See next chapter for detailed consideration.

[18] *Ibid.*, p. 106.

the Balkan peoples, and to inaugurate an era of production and durable peace, it is essential to abolish all obstacles to friendly relations by the conclusion of a Pact on a basis of equality and equity as between the Balkan peoples, which would strengthen existing treaties by additional guarantees of security : (1) reiterates the recommendation of the first Balkan Conference in favour of a Pact to outlaw war and to provide for arbitration and mutual assistance (2) instructs the Council to submit to a Committee of Inquiry the preliminary draft of the Balkan Pact put forward by the Greek delegation, as also the proposals for ensuring the loyal execution of the minority and other clauses of the peace treaties ; and to consider what steps can be taken to deal with situations likely to hinder the moral disarmament of the Balkan peoples. The Committee shall submit to the next Conference a final report which shall be circulated to the national groups three months before the meeting of the said Conference." [19]

The second resolution was intimately connected with the first.

"The Conference : Pending the drafting of the Balkan Pact : (1) calls attention to the vital importance of the earliest possible conclusion between the Governments of the Balkan nations of a multi-lateral pact of arbitration and friendship ; (2) adopts the recommendation of the Council of the Conference in favour of the establishment of direct relations between the national groups of the parties concerned, in order to reach agreement on matters likely to endanger good relations between them and to ensure scrupulous respect for all obligations arising out of treaties now in force, including those dealing with the protection of minorities." [20]

[19] League of Nations, *Bulletin of Information on the Work of International Organization*, Vol. IV, No. 1, March 1932, p. 12.
[20] *Ibid.*

The other two resolutions urged success on the Disarmament Conference, and renewed the plea that the foreign ministers of the several states meet annually.[21]

The other commissions were able to make greater progress than the Political Commission, partly because their agenda related to specific rather than general issues, and partly because the questions involved technical and expert analysis rather than political oratory. The great danger in international organization lies not so much in the possible failure of the organization to protect or further the real interests of the people, as it does in the possibility that constructive steps will be hindered or rendered impossible as a result of partisan contention and loss of face among the orators on the political questions.

Having canvassed the general economic situation at the first Conference, the Economics Commission confined itself to the development of specific projects likely to lead to an amelioration of the situation. Statutes establishing the Balkan Chamber of Commerce and Industry at Istanbul were examined and adopted.[22] Resolutions were adopted urging the creation of a Balkan Chamber of Agriculture modeled after the Chamber of Commerce and Industry, a Central Cereal Office to co-ordinate production, distribution, and sales, an Inter-Balkan Grain Exchange, a Central Tobacco Office, and a Central Union of Co-operative Societies.[23]

The Communications Commission continued its study of methods of developing Balkan communications along

---

[21] *Survey of International Affairs*, 1931, p. 338.
[22] Papanastassiou, *op. cit.*, p. 112.
[23] *Ibid.*, pp. 111-113.

lines of need and utility in place of military strategy.[24] The Commission examined in greater detail the suggestions of the former Conference that two inter-Balkan trunk lines be built — the one to run north-south, the other east-west. Progress was made but a need was felt for expert engineering advice, and the matter was put over until the third Conference for final disposition with the request that such experts examine the situation prior to that time and be present at the Conference to discuss it.

For immediate action the Conference recommended : building two bridges over the Danube, one for the route between Bucharest and Sofia, the other for that between Bucharest and Belgrade ; rebuilding the narrow-gauge road in the Struma Valley, and building a road on the Greek side to open a direct line between Sofia and Athens via Salonika ; improvement of the existing Salonika-Istanbul line, transit of which now requires the absurd length of 25 hours ; construction of a line in both Albania and Greece connecting Durazzo-Tirana-Salonika.[25] At the suggestion of the Greek delegation it was voted by the Conference that the Balkan Postal Union should begin operation as soon as two states ratified the protocol. The door was left open for other states to adhere at any time.[26]

The Committee on Intellectual Co-operation urged the creation of an Institute of Historical Research at Istanbul. The recommendation of the last Conference

---

[24] See G. P. Banyankas, *Considérations générales au sujet de l'amélioration de la Communication Ferroviare Interbalkanique*, Athens, 1931.

[25] 2ème Conférence Balkanique, *Raccordements des Chemins de Fer Balkaniques*, Athens, 1931, p. 6.

[26] Mimeographed Report of the Plenary Session of the 2nd Conference, 23rd October, 1931, *Agence Anatolie*, Istanbul, 1931, p. 3 ; Papanastassiou, *op. cit.*, p. 117.

for a multilateral extradition treaty was also renewed.[27]

The Committee on Health and Social Policy advocated the creation of a Balkan Bureau of Sanitary Information at Istanbul for the exchange and publication of statistics and information concerning conditions of health in the Balkans. It also recommended the creation of a Balkan Labour Office, modeled after and associated with the International Labour Office. The unification of social legislation was favoured. After reviewing the status of married women, it was proposed that they should retain their original nationality until naturalized.[28]

The closing session of the Conference was held at Ankara where the delegates were received and addressed by the President of the Republic. In his speech Mustapha Kemal Pasha said that while Balkan history recorded many unhappy and painful events, all states including Turkey shared in it, and he hailed the Conference for submerging the unfortunate memories of the past and for opening the way to a happier and sounder future. "The only way of making people happy is energetic action which seeks to unite them to make them love one another and to mutually assure them of their material and moral needs. I am persuaded that your initiative tending to facilitate general understanding will engender an eminently humanitarian attitude and will serve world peace."

III

THE second Conference went far to demonstrate the sincerity and acceptability of the movement launched

---

[27] Papanastassiou, *op. cit.*, pp. 113-114.
[28] *Ibid.*, p. 116.

in 1930. In the preparation for the Conference, in the quality and number of delegates, in the spirit of the sessions, and in the interest taken by the governments, the second Conference marked an advance over its predecessor. Constructive progress was made by all Commissions, save possibly the Political. And even with respect to the labours and controversies of that Commission, credit must be given for the avoidance of a complete breakdown, the maintenance of friendly collaboration, and the agreement calling for continued study. These are evidences of deft statesmanship, sincerity, and a genuine desire to substitute order for chaos. The continued search for means of promoting the general welfare of all the Balkan peoples merits highest praise and gives promise of significant results. As cogently stated by the leading spirit behind the movement, it "inspires the conviction that if the work of the Conference is carried forward with equal success and if the inter-Balkan organizations envisaged are put into operation, some day we will find ourselves in Union without having perceived how we arrived there." [29]

IV

WHEN the Council met at Istanbul on the 28th January, 1932, it was faced with the fact that nothing had been done since the dissolution of the Conference to give effect to its actions ; that the strained relations between Bulgaria and Yugoslavia were worse rather than better ; and that the economic crisis was stretching its withering tentacles more and more into the Balkans. [30] The

[29] Papanastassiou, *op. cit.*, p. 120.
[30] See review of the trade situation in *Le Messager d'Athènes*, 11th October, 1932 ; *Les Balkans*, Athens, December-January 1932, pp. 231-247.

Council was, therefore, confronted with the task of discovering some way of circumventing the barriers to progress and union so that unanimous recommendations might be presented to the next Conference.

The greater part of the Council's working time was spent considering the projected Balkan pact and the minorities issue as raised by the Bulgarians, in order that the next Conference might be spared the destructive contentiousness which had prevailed at the second Conference. Five amendments were worked out and added to the pact as originally proposed by Professor Spiropoulos. The amendments provided for : (1) the creation in each state of a Minorities Commission ; (2) the creation of an inter-Balkan Minorities Commission which would sit annually in each state to review the actions of the national commissions and to entertain petitions and grievances ; (3) the execution of the commissions' awards by the states ; (4) the faithful support of the state by minorities ; and (5) the taking of all steps for the suppression of actions likely to trouble the peace or the good relations between states.[31]

These amendments represented, in substance, an attempt to resolve the fundamental controversies between Bulgaria and her neighbors. Many of the phrases are outright concessions to Bulgaria, but not all. Article 21 seeks to satisfy her by requiring her neighbours to admit that they have not carried out their commitments regarding minorities, and by requiring them to undertake another obligation. Articles 22-25 strengthen the obligation by the institution of new machinery in addition to that provided for by the League

---

[31] *Les Balkans*, September 1932, p. 701 ; Papanastassiou, *op. cit.*, pp. 251-253 ; *L'Esprit International*, April 1932, pp. 218-221.

of Nations, of which by 1934 all Balkan states were members. The theory justifying the erection of more organization is apparently that the League is too remote, and that these new devices, being home-made and intimate affairs, will more readily comprehend the situations, be able to suggest Balkan solutions, and be able to command greater respect by the states. Article 26, on the other hand, is an equally important concession to Bulgaria's neighbours, as well as to all Balkan states harbouring foreign groups. It specifies that minorities must be loyal to the state of their residence and abstain from all actions directed against the state. Here Yugoslavian, Greek, and Rumanian diplomacy can find ample substantiation for the claim that heretofore such groups have not so conducted themselves, and that the states will henceforth have something more of a legal right to take steps against minorities not behaving properly. But the second paragraph is the more significant. The provocative and disturbing agency in Bulgarian-Yugoslavian relations has been the Internal Macedonian Revolutionary Organization, which has as its goal an independent Macedonian state or secondarily the incorporation of all Macedonians in an enlarged Bulgarian territory. For years Yugoslavia has insisted, and rightly, that a prelude to reconciliation with Bulgaria must involve suppression of armed bands raiding or terrorizing Yugoslavian Macedonia from Bulgarian territory.[32] Bulgaria has disclaimed responsibility for the conduct of these bands or professed herself powerless to suppress them. Bulgarian acceptance of this pact

[32] See the case of the *Caroline* in Wharton, *Digest of International Law*, Vol. I, sec. 50 ; Pitt-Cobbett, *Leading Cases on International Law*, Vol. I, pp. 168-169 ; J. B. Moore, *Digest of International Law*, Vol. II, sec. 217.

would make her legally and morally responsible for their actions.

The loyal execution of these provisions should do much to remove one of Europe's most cancerous situations. But the primary consideration is their adoption. Each side will be reluctant to accept, for the finger of accusation is but thinly veiled, and diplomacy is not fond of "losing face." But, in the mutual give and take which is involved lies the only philosophy upon which this or any other international dispute can be settled without the inauguration of new grievances.

After agreeing upon these propositions concerning the political questions, the Council drew up the agenda for the next Conference.[33] It was agreed that during the Balkan Week in the spring, conferences should be held on social questions at Sofia, medical questions at Athens, "tourism" and intellectual co-operation at Bucharest, commerce and industry at Istanbul, and unification of laws at Belgrade.[34] The balance of the Council's time was so occupied with feasting and social affairs[35]— that essential part of any international organization — that it did not hear the report of the Commission on Juridical questions, nor did it form any of the eighteen committees provided for in resolutions of the preceding Conference.[36] The Council adjourned January 31st, having received little notice by the press and having accomplished but one important act, which, unfortunately, was to lead to greater dissension in the ensuing Conference.

Disquieted by the turmoil which the Conference de-

[33] See pages 48-49 *postea.*
[34] *Les Balkans,* February-March 1932, p. 324.
[35] *Near East and India,* 10th March, 1932, p. 201.
[36] *Ibid.*

bates upon political issues had caused, misconstruing the real motives of the movement, and perhaps envious, but at least suspicious of the efforts being exerted to solve the political and ethnic clashes, Foreign Ministers Marinkovitch of Yugoslavia and Michalakopoulos of Greece announced to the Balkan press at the time of the League Council in March 1932, that the Balkan Conferences should abstain from touching political questions. In defence of the movement, M. Papanastassiou asserted that there are no matters today which do not impinge upon political questions. Peoples have as much right to discuss the things which concern themselves as governments. They want peace, conciliation, good relations, as much as governments do, and they have requested their governments to take action in the past but the governments have not seen fit to do so. Far from hindering the governments, said M. Papanastassiou, the work of the Conference really facilitates them, if they have the well-being of their peoples in mind. However, the Conferences have never undertaken to bind the governments without their consent.[37]

While this reply served to silence outspoken governmental opposition, the destructive attitude displayed by these spokesmen was but the beginning of a rocky year for the movement. Balkan Weeks were held in only three capitals. At Istanbul the inter-Balkan Chamber of Commerce and Industry was opened. At Athens a medical conference was held and the doctors founded a Balkan Hygiene Association.[38] At Belgrade a conference of jurists to consider unification of laws was convened. Bulgarian representatives refused to attend

[37] *Le Messager d'Athènes,* 21st March, 1932.
[38] *Les Balkans,* August 1932, p. 569.

the conferences in Athens and Belgrade,[39] and the jurists had to adjourn noting that "obviously the Commission can make little advance under present conditions."[40] Three other conferences met, but not as parts of Balkan Weeks. A tobacco conference was held at Istanbul which resulted in the decision to set up a Balkan Tobacco Office "entrusted with the task of preparing the settlement of all outstanding questions;"[41] a conference of co-operative societies met at Bucharest but adjourned without having taken any important decision.[42] The most discouraging of the conferences was, however, the inter-Balkan university conference held in Sofia in July. Turkey refused to send any representatives; and the Rumanian delegates voiced considerable displeasure that the next Balkan Conference was to meet at Bucharest.[43]

The Chamber of Commerce and Industry deserves a note in passing, for its foundation in the midst of an economic crisis emphasizing nationalism is significant of the new spirit developing in the Balkans. According to the statute establishing it,[44] the Chamber exists to : (1) facilitate and encourage intimate economic relations between all of the Balkan states ; (2) ameliorate the conditions under which commerce and industry are carried on ; (3) organize fairs, expositions, and museums ; (4) improve relations between capital and labour ; (5) help develop an inter-Balkan conscience ;

[39] Papanastassiou, *Vers L'Union Balkanique,* p. 126.

[40] *Near East and India,* 23rd June, 1932, p. 500.

[41] *Near East and India,* 9th June, 1932, p. 461; *Bulgarian-British Review,* Sofia, October 1932, p. 2 ; *Le Messager d'Athènes,* 2nd September, 1933.

[42] *Les Balkans,* April-May 1932, p. 380.

[43] *The Near East and India,* 28th July, 1932, p. 601.

[44] *Les Balkans,* August 1932.

(6) bring about arbitration of all economic, commercial, and industrial disputes. Such a programme is an ambitious one, but necessarily so with Balkan trade constituting but 9 per cent of the trade of the Balkan states. The establishment of this institution marks one more step in the evolution of an ideal. But the attainment of the ideal must involve more than the simple creation of institutions, for these easily become ends in themselves losing sight of the larger goal of which they are but a part. While the inauguration of these various chambers and bureaus is laudable, their eventual justification must lie in the degree to which they contribute to the attainment of the ultimate ideal. The justification must be in action as well as in statutes.[45]

[45] See good article on the Chamber in *Les Balkans*, August 1932, pp. 564-569.

CHAPTER THREE

HESITATION

I

PRIOR to the opening of the third Conference at Bucharest, a series of unfortunate events transpired. It will be recalled that at the second Conference a suggestion was adopted that bi-partite conferences be held during the year.[1] The Bulgarians proposed a series of such conferences, but only the Albanians responded. The Albanians and Bulgarians signed a protocol for the complete application of the minorities treaties.[2] In the latter part of September, the Bulgarian group asked that the Conference be postponed since no steps had been taken to solve the minorities issue or to carry out the above suggestion.[3] This proposal was not agreed to, inasmuch as there had been no order that such negotiations must precede the convocation of the third Conference,[4] and inasmuch as the Conference statutes called for a meeting every October.[5] The Bulgarian delegation shortly thereafter announced its intention of not participating in the Conference. It was eventually prevailed upon to attend after assurances had been given

[1] Page 31 *ante*.

[2] *Les Balkans*, December-January 1932, p. 208.

[3] Papanastassiou, *Vers*, p. 126; *Bulgarian-British Review*, October 1932, p. 2.

[4] *Le Messager d'Athènes*, 9th November, 1932.

[5] Papanastassiou, "*La Troisième Conférence Balkanique*," *Les Balkans*, October-November 1932, p. 5 ; Papanastassiou, *Vers*, p. 127.

that bi-party negotiations would take place after the Conference.[6]   However, the small delegation that came brought instructions demanding as the price of attendance early consideration of the minorities problem[7] which led the Athenian journal *Elefthéron Vima* to remark that such action was not calculated to advance the Balkans toward their objective, but rather to endanger the entire edifice. The paper admonished the Bulgarians that such a delicate question could not be resolved at one meeting, but that a sincere and protracted endeavour was necessary.[8]   To make matters worse, a fresh series of violent frontier incidents broke out along the Bulgar-Yugoslavian boundary.[9]

Actions casting doubt over the fate of the coming Conference were not confined to the Bulgarians.   Rumanian politics experienced an attack of convulsions, leaving in question until the last moment the personalities who would come in contact with the Conference, and the tone that the country would assume toward co-operation.   More embarrassing even was a public announcement by Rumania's notable historian, Professor Iorga, that after all, Bulgaria was the only Balkan country, that Rumania had nothing in common with nor desired to have anything to do with Balkan questions : she was a European power.[10] However, the Rumanian delegation immediately caused a notice to be published in every Balkan newspaper expressing the joy of the Rumanians in having the Conference meet at Bucharest.   "In the desire of a sincere *rapprochement,* and convinced that

[6] *Les Balkans,* October-November 1932, p. 6.
[7] *The Near East and India,* 27th October, 1932.
[8] *Le Messager d'Athènes,* 15th October, 1932.
[9] *The Near East and India,* 3rd November, 1932, p. 880.
[10] *Ibid.,* 17th November, 1932, p. 923.

the Balkan States are allied not only by the tradition of a common life in the past but as much by common interests in the future, we anticipate the reunion of the delegates of the five States of the Peninsula with the firm desire for entente and amity." [11]

The gathering storm clouds became more evident at a session of the Council on October 21st, immediately preceding the Conference. The Bulgarians seized the floor at the opening of the Council and expressed regret that the action of the last Conference respecting minorities had not been carried out. [12] They then presented a formal letter proposing that the Conference be postponed until the following spring in order to carry out the wishes of the last Conference. While recognizing that the amended draft-pact accorded a certain amount of recognition to their claims, they called attention to the fact that the governments had done nothing so far to carry out the proposals of the Conferences. On the other hand, referring without specification to the actions of Foreign Ministers Marinkovitch and Michalakopoulos at Geneva in March, they charged that by clever devices the governments were sidetracking all political issues, and they, therefore, saw no point in going on when the states were no nearer conciliation and settlement. [13]

The Council bowed before an apparent impasse and contented itself with taking account of the declaration and affirming unanimously the previous suggestion for bilateral political negotiations. After adding an item to the agenda for consideration of the possibility of

[11] *Les Balkans*, October-November 1932, p. 72.
[12] *Ibid.*, p. 73.
[13] *Ibid.*, pp. 73-77.

erecting monuments to slain soldiers in the War, the Council adjourned.[14]

II

ALTHOUGH the convocation was thus accompanied by the rapid accumulation of storm clouds, the opening plenary session was brilliant and cordial. The Conference assembled under the benevolent presidency of M. Stefan Ciceo-Pop, President of the Rumanian Chamber of Deputies, who warmly welcomed the delegates to Bucharest and pledged the loyal co-operation and endeavour of the Rumanian national group.[15] Foreign Minister Titulescu saluted the assemblage and their cause, saying that Rumania did not hesitate to support the work of the Conference ; that their efforts, far from impeding the governments, facilitated their actions ; and that a solidarity of interest was developing that would not remain fruitless.[16]

Such a statement was a hopeful antidote for the pessimistic announcements served up before the Conference. While it may be true that certain governments have done more by way of lip service than actual work for the cause of Balkan union, M. Titulescu's activities behind the scenes of the Conference and during the ensuing years have tended to demonstrate that the Rumanian Government is willing to lend a greater degree of support than her famous historian indicated.

Speeches by the group leaders followed. While refraining from provocative and overly contentious lan-

---

[14] *Les Balkans*, October-November 1932, p. 78.

[15] *Le Messager d'Athènes*, 15th October, 1932.

[16] *Les Balkans*, October-November 1932, pp. 79-80 ; *Le Messager d'Athènes*, 23rd October, 1932.

guage, the speeches nevertheless showed a preliminary jockeying for position. M. Pop, host to the Conference, and therefore under obligation to be as impartial as possible, emphasized that a Balkan entente would be directed at no country, within or without the peninsula. The minorities issue must be settled as a part of the larger pacification and be based upon principles of equity and right.[17] M. Konitza of Albania stated that the success would depend not only on what was done in the Conferences but upon what the delegations did with their governments. He stated that the Albanian group could see no reason to participate any longer in the Conferences if the draft pact were not adopted before the next Conference. The adoption of the pact would present a definite opportunity to the governments to show their real attitude on peace and co-operation.[18] M. Trifonoff of Bulgaria reiterated the traditional Bulgarian theme, saying that there could be no union until all individuals and groups were accorded free and equal rights, and that the Bulgarians regretted that the Conferences had not done more to solve the problem. A conciliatory note was struck when he added that the Bulgarians were convinced that the minorities questions could not be solved by war, and that the Bulgarians were genuinely sincere in their profession for union and co-operation.[19] M. Papanastassiou, after reviewing the measures taken in Greece to carry on the movement, pointed out the similarity between the Balkan and the League meetings in the opportunities which

[17] *Les Balkans*, October-November 1932, pp. 81-86.
[18] *Ibid.*, p. 87.
[19] *Ibid.*, pp. 88-89.

were afforded statesmen to discuss informally issues that could not be touched in special *ad hoc* conferences because of the attendant publicity.[20] M. Hassan Bey's speech was energetic and enthusiastic. He said the time had come to move from desires to realities. Union, said the Turkish leader, was a necessity as well as an ideal.[21] M. Yovanovitch's speech was brief and strictly in line with the traditional Yugoslavian policy that the solution of political questions must wait upon the prior disposal of other issues.[22]

From a tactical point of view, the situation at the opening of the Conference would appear to have been as follows : The Bulgarians and Yugoslavians remained entrenched in the positions taken up at the second Conference. The Greeks, Rumanians, and Turks remained in the open field primarily interested in advancing Balkan union from all possible angles and possessing no grievances demanding prior settlement. The Albanians sought to appear favouring the Greek, Rumanian, and Turk attitude, but in reality they sought to use their power to force an immediate solution of the Bulgar-Yugoslav problem favourable to Bulgaria. The Conference was thus divided into two groups, but not irreconcilable groups, since the Greek-Rumanian-Turk combination was in a position and an attitude to provide mediation for the conflict taking place within the other group.

The agenda for the Conference provided for consideration of the following items :

---

[20] *Les Balkans*, October-November 1932, pp. 89-93.
[21] *Ibid.*, pp. 93-95.
[22] *Ibid.*, pp. 95-96.

I (1) Adoption of rules of procedure for the Conferences and Commissions.

(2) Application of resolutions of second Conference, and the creation of commissions provided for by the resolutions.

(3) Examination of the propositions of the Commission on Intellectual *Rapprochement*.

II (1) The Balkan Pact of Union.

III (1) The statutes for the Institute of Historical Research.

(2) Development of a manual of Balkan history.

(3) Translations of literature and drama.

(4) Balkan films.

(5) Collaboration of radio broadcasting.

(6) Collaboration of the press.

IV (1) Convention concerning partial customs union.

(2) Statute for a Chamber of Agriculture.

(3) Collaboration regarding agricultural and agronomic research.

(4) Collaboration in the development of agricultural credit.

V (1) Development of communications and transport, including a Balkan Maritime Office at Istanbul.

(2) Project of co-operation in building highways and railroads.

(3) Prolongation of roads from termini of railways to facilitate connections between capitals.

(4) Establishment of a plan of public works.

(5) Aërial communications.

VI (1) Convention for aliens.

(2) Statute for an Inter-Balkan Labour Office.

(3) Charter of rights for women and children.

(4) Legislation regarding married women.
(5) Sanitary and veterinary convention.
(6) Common action against tuberculosis.[23]

III

ALTHOUGH all of the group leaders had approved of
the draft pact of union at the Council session in
January, the incidents preceding the Conference left
little doubt but that the debate in the Political Commission would produce trouble. The debate was
started by the Bulgarians who demanded that Article
21, which provided that "In order to render more effective the protection of minorities, the contracting Parties,
on the basis of the respective clauses of the treaties
concerning the minorities . . . take the following
obligations," should be so altered as to make clear that
the term "minorities" included groupings based on
"race, language, and religion as well as national conscience."[24]   M. Spiropoulos, the reporter, and M. Yovanovitch of Yugoslavia countered by urging that the
definition of minorities be left to the treaties originally
providing for their status in order that there might not
be confusion of terms ; while M. Papanastassiou argued
that it would be wisest to permit science and practice
to determine the constituent elements of nationality.[25]
Having again met rebuff on the minorities issue, at
the second session of the Commission M. Trifonoff of
Bulgaria proposed an adjournment of the debate until
the next Conference in order to permit the carrying out

---

[23] *Les Balkans*, February-March 1932, p. 324 ; *Programme*, Comité
Roumain chargé d'Organiser la Conférence, Bucharest 1932 ; *Le Messager
d'Athènes*, 8th October, 1932.
[24] *Les Balkans*, October-November 1932, p. 99.
[25] *Ibid.*

of the bilateral negotiations, adding the threat that
if this were not agreed to, the delegation would find
itself obliged to withdraw from the Conference.[26]
The Rumanian and Greek representatives remonstrated
with the Bulgarians, seeking to point out, as they had
before, that the Conference was a private affair and
could not bind the governments, that it was futile to
adjourn a private conference because the governments
had not carried out a specific suggestion, and that Bulgarian withdrawal would only complicate the conciliatory efforts of the Conference, as well as throw into
doubt the real attitude of Bulgaria.[27] The Albanian
delegation then revealed its position. It demanded an
immediate vote on the matter, saying that it came with
a mandate for adoption or else for withdrawal from the
Conference.[28] A meeting of the Council was held and
it was voted to proceed with the debate, whereupon
the Albanians and Bulgarians withdrew from the Conference meetings, though remaining in the city.[29] Despite this action, characterized by one periodical "as
an act of folly and short-sighted intransigeance," the
Conference continued its labours according to schedule.
Before the Albanians and Bulgarians quit Bucharest, it
appears that the Greeks and Rumanians agreed to discuss the issue with them privately after the Conference,
and to use their good office to reconcile the Yugoslavs.[30]

The Yugoslavian group had been content at the second session to withhold any statement of its policy. At

[26] *Les Balkans*, October-November 1932, p. 100 ; Papanastassiou, *op. cit.*,
p. 128.

[27] Papanastassiou, *op. cit.*, p. 129.

[28] *Ibid.*, p. 129 ; *Les Balkans*, October-November 1932, p. 100.

[29] Papanastassiou, *op. cit.*, p. 130 ; *Les Balkans*, *supra*, p. 102.

[30] *Le Messager d'Athènes*, 4th January, 1934, p. 6.

the third session, however, it came to the fore. It insisted that the existing treaties and the League of Nations offered all possible guarantees respecting minorities and that to add more, as under the proposed Articles 21-26, would merely stimulate turbulent and revolutionary groups. It therefore proposed the following in place of Articles 23-25: "It is left to the competence of the diplomatic conference between the Balkan countries to examine the means of rendering the protection of minorities as efficacious as possible within the structure of the existing treaties." [31] This new proposal was voted down 20-5, it being the majority opinion that the organization provided for in Articles 21-26 would facilitate the Entente, provide additional security for the minorities, and not interfere with the competence of the League of Nations or the work of the governments. Above all, to discard these articles, it was maintained, would be to place matters back where they had been at the second Conference.[32]

In reporting the draft pact to the third plenary session, M. Spiropoulos said that the pact must be looked at as a whole, and one part must not be emphasized to the detriment of the rest. The Committee, he said, favoured the pact as a whole, although it disagreed on certain parts. He moved its adoption by the Conference, suggesting that amendments be made after the adoption of the complete instrument.[33] On this suggestion the Conference submerged differences relative to the details and unanimously adopted the draft pact.[34]

---

[31] Papanastassiou, *op. cit.*, p. 131 ; *Les Balkans, supra*, p. 103.

[32] *Ibid.*, pp. 131-132 ; *Les Balkans, supra*, p. 184.

[33] *Les Balkans*, October-November 1932, pp. 146-153 ; *ibid.*, December, 1932, pp. 291-294.

[34] *Ibid.* October-November 1932, p. 153 ; Papanastassiou, *op. cit.*, p. 132.

The draft pact, which may be found in the Appendix,[34a] contains a preamble, and thirty-nine articles divided between five chapters. The preamble, containing the customary lofty expressions regarding peace, security, solidarity and reconciliation, expressed the "desire of applying in the fullest possible manner the system provided for in the Covenant of the League of Nations for the peaceful settlement of the differences between the Balkan States, of affording further guarantees of safety within the framework of existing treaties, including those concerning the protection of minorities." Chapter One relating to non-aggression and amity provides that the parties shall not "attack nor invade" one another, nor have "recourse in any case to war" against another contractant, but shall submit "all questions of whatever nature they may be" to pacific settlement, with the exception of three significant exemptions—(1) the exercise of the right of legitimate self-defence, (2) action taken in the application of Article XVI of the Covenant of the League of Nations ; and (3) an action resulting from a decision of the Assembly or Council of the League of Nations, or in the application of Article XV, paragraph 7 of the Covenant of the League of Nations, provided that in the last instance that action is directed against a State which has first been subject to an attack." The parties further agree to take all steps to see that "the obligations flowing from" the treaties shall be applied.

Chapter Two containing the provisions relative to the pacific settlement of disputes is divided into the usual two sections dealing with conciliation, and judicial or arbitral settlement. One of the most noteworthy pro-

[34a] Appendix I.

visions regarding conciliation is to be found in Article 3 which exempts from any conciliation procedure unsettled disputes concerning the territorial *status quo* of the parties, or questions left by international law to the "exclusive jurisdiction of States." Conciliation is to be accomplished through a Permanent Conciliation Commission made up exclusively of representatives of the contracting parties. The provisions governing the submission and conciliation of disputes are the customary ones found more or less in the same form in the majority of conciliation agreements drawn up since the war.[35] Appeal to the Permanent Court of International Justice, in case of dissatisfaction with the decision of the Conciliation Commission is preferred to arbitration in the section dealing with judicial or arbitral settlement. Appeal is to lie to the Court unless the parties agree to submit to an arbitral tribunal.

Chapter Three provides for mutual assistance in case of violation of the non-aggression compact found in Chapter One. Violations are to be submitted to the Council of the League which is authorized to act on a four-fifths vote, the parties excluded. The contracting parties agree, upon the suggestions of the Council of the League, "to go immediately to the assistance of the Power against which the unlawful action has been directed," a somewhat more specific undertaking than that called for in mutual assistance conventions which prescribe that steps shall be taken against "the aggressor," which is not always nor easily determined. In instances of "flagrant violation" of the compact, such as the crossing of the frontier, or the opening of hos-

[35] See Habicht, M., *Post-War Treaties for the Pacific Settlement of International Disputes*, Cambridge, 1931.

tilities, immediate action by the other states is demanded
when the aggrieved party establishes the fact that the
"violation constitutes an unprovoked act of aggression"
and that urgent measures are demanded.   In this event,
however, the League is still to be seized of the question,
and shall advise the parties of its decision.

Chapter Four deals with the protection of minorities.
It was adopted in the form recommended by the preceding Council and needs no further comment here.[35a]

The last chapter is devoted to general provisions.   It
makes allowance for methods of settlement already provided for by existing treaties, for possible conflicts between appeals to the Conciliation Commission or the
Permanent Court of International Justice, for provisional orders of the settlement agencies, for disputes
involving third parties, for differences arising from the
interpretation of the pact.   Finally, Article 36 in Chapter Five states that nothing in the pact shall be interpreted as interfering with the duty of the League in
preserving peace, or with the obligations of the participants under the Covenant of the League.

As an agreement looking toward the pacific settlement
of differences, the draft pact is highly interesting.   But
as a pact of union, as popularly hailed, it is disappoint-
ing.   Taken as a whole, there is very little that is novel
and much that is questionable.   A comparison with the
Little Entente's General Act of Conciliation, Arbitration and Judicial Settlement, reproduced in the Appendix,[35b] will reveal that a large part of the conference
proposal has been copied from or suggested by it.
Twenty-six of the thirty-nine articles are the same, or

[35a] See pages 36-37 *ante.*
[35b] See Appendix II.

substantially the same as those in the Little Entente General Act, although their arrangement and placing may be different.

The provisions concerning non-aggression and amity are copied directly from Article 1 of the Græco-Rumanian Treaty of the 21st March, 1928[36] and Article 2 of the Græco-Yugoslavian Treaty of the 27th March, 1929.[37] While such provisions are not incompatible with the Kellogg-Briand Pact, as was made clear in the exchange of notes among the signatories of that Pact,[38] they do mark a definite recession from its advanced position. In this respect, therefore, the draft pact enjoys no claim to uniqueness ; although, considering Balkan history, any compact which would bind the Balkan powers to forego the utilization of war against one another would mark a major advance for the cause of peace.

Articles 2 and 21 seek to reach down to the fundamental difficulties of the states in calling upon the signatories to admit laxity in enforcing treaty commitments. The acceptance of these provisions by the states may be doubted. Diplomacy does not customarily relish frank avowals of failure. However, the adoption of such principles is important, and even necessary for a complete *rapprochement*.

Article 3, in Chapter Two, and Article 34 in Chapter Five, do not represent a continuation of this spirit. The exclusion of questions relating to the territorial status from conciliation and judicial examination is not new. In fact, the provisions of Article 3 are lifted

[36] League of Nations, *Treaty Series*, Vol. 108, p. 189.

[37] *Ibid.*, Vol. 108, p. 205.

[38] *American Journal of International Law, Official Documents*, January 1929, pp. 1-13.

directly from the Czechoslovak-Polish Treaty of the 23rd April, 1925,[39] the Greek-Rumanian Treaty of the 21st March, 1928,[40] and the Greek-Yugoslav Treaty of the 27th March, 1929.[41]   It is one thing to exempt from the machinery of pacific settlement questions relating to the territorial status of states not bordering, nor ever likely to, upon one another.   It is similarly one thing to exclude from conciliation such questions when both states emerged victors on the same side from a world war.   But it is an entirely different thing to make such exemptions in a multi-lateral treaty linking states which do harbour definite grievances as a result of hasty and partial peace settlements.   It is pertinent to note, in this connection, that Article 1 of the Little Entente General Act does not contain any such exemption. The insertion of such clauses in the light of the universally-known claims of Bulgaria, and even more in the presence of Bulgarian withdrawal from the Conference upon just such a territorial issue, is a return to the old, unhappy policies.   It is a move hardly calculated to draw Bulgaria closer into the circle, and one entirely out of keeping with the principle of *rapprochement* and union.   To be sure, Bulgaria retains her right to appeal to the League of Nations for revision in accordance with Article 19 of the Covenant.   But the draft pact, in the words of the Conference resolution, is supposed to be an additional and more effective instrument for ensuring peace, providing that this is not interpreted here nor in the preamble as a "victor's peace."   Even viewing the pact as a whole, without giving undue em-

---

[39] League of Nations, *Treaty Series*, Vol. 48, p. 386.

[40] *Ibid.*, Vol. 108, p. 191.

[41] *Ibid.*, Vol. 108, p. 205.

phasis to any part or clause, it cannot be expected that these ends will be satisfactorily achieved so long as it has such exemptions as are contained in the first parts of Article 3 and Article 34. If Balkan statesmen have not learned that the seeking of unfair and unequal advantages is incompatible with the establishment of a permanent structure of peace, the movement for federation and union is doomed from the start, and the Balkan people may anticipate a return to the conditions prevailing during their unfortunate past. No state can be tied by a non-employment-of-force contract and at the same time justifiably be denied the right to seek a peaceful or judicial solution of its grievances.

The machinery and procedure of conciliation and pacific settlement follows the Hague Convention of 1907, the Covenant of the League of Nations, and post-war treaties for conciliation and pacific settlement. It is not as perfect as Article 8 of the Little Entente treaty which says that "all disputes . . . shall be submitted obligatorily to a procedure of conciliation." In providing in Article 4 that the conciliation commissions shall be composed of representatives of the Balkan states alone, the parties are taking another step to exclude foreign influence from the peninsula. While this may be an admirable idea, one questions whether the point has been reached where the Balkan states alone can settle by conciliation and without the aid of a neutral party questions which diplomacy has failed to resolve. It would seem wiser to amend Article 4 and permit the conciliation commission to call in, at least on certain occasions and for a time, an outside authority, as is the case with the Little Entente.

Serious question pertains to the complete freedom

that is left to the states in the indefinite appointment
and removal of conciliators.   By virtue of this it would
be possible for contesting states to shuffle their representatives, and to get friendly nations to do the same, so as
to defeat all possibility of conciliation.

The section dealing with judicial and arbitral settlement is not so strong as might be desired.   It fails to
reflect some of the progress made in this field since the
war.   Neither arbitration nor judicial settlement is
compulsory.   There is nothing automatic in the system.
If conciliation breaks down, pacific settlement stops at
that point unless one of the parties "requests" procedure before the World Court.   If it is desired to end
all employment of force, and to render peace more secure, this section should be strengthened by the
addition of provisions which will automatically and
immediately call into action arbitration and/or judicial
settlement.   To leave an interval of three months between the breakdown of negotiations for the establishment of an arbitration tribunal and appeal to the
Permanent Court of International Justice would, in
many serious and inflammatory cases, be disastrous to
peace.   While, apart from the exemptions noted earlier,
the provisions relating to non-aggression and mutual
assistance (Chapter Three) are fairly satisfactory, it
is not enough to pledge the parties to non-aggression
and leave flaws in the settlement machinery.   Too much
uncertainty remains as to the meaning and nature of
"aggression" and measures of "legitimate self-defence."
Non-aggression agreements must be accompanied by
settlement machinery as nearly perfect as possible.

The minorities provisions have already been com-
mented upon above, and require no further attention

at this point as they were adopted in the form recommended at the January Council meeting.

Well might the delegates exclaim "Habemus Pactum." Although the draft pact failed to provide for federation or union, failed to utilize the most advanced forms of organization and treaty drafting, and although it is open to numerous criticisms, nevertheless its adoption is significant. If it seemed to lag behind the more advanced ideas of co-operation evidenced in the resolutions of the other commissions, it should not be forgotten that the gravest differences between the Balkan peoples have been the political ones. The first steps in life, whether individual or corporate, are always the most difficult. Experience perfects the initial effort.

After the adoption of the draft by the Conference, the Bulgarian group issued a declaration to the press, stating that it would do all that was possible to adhere to the pact,[42] thus ending the political work of the Conference with a note of hope.

IV

THE Economic Commission at the third Conference dealt with questions involving a convention for a customs union, statutes for an inter-Balkan Chamber of Agriculture, collaboration in scientific, agricultural, and agronomic research, and co-operation in providing agricultural credit.

The Commission noted in its discussions that its most difficult problem was that of finding a basis for economic collaboration. All countries are primarily agricultural, producing nearly the same commodities, seeking exports to the same markets, and importing

[42] Papanastassiou, *Vers L'Union Balkanique*, p. 132.

relatively little from one another. Greece, the principal importer of other Balkan goods, supplies only grapes, tobacco, and luxuries, all of which the other states also produce. Bulgaria, Rumania, and Yugoslavia are dependent upon the export of cereals and grains for securing foreign exchange, and their needs are for manufactured or semi-manufactured goods, which none of the Balkan states are in a position to supply.[43]

There was considerable discussion of a Chamber of Agriculture to exchange information, organize activities to fight pests and diseases, stimulate fairs and exhibitions, study the unification of agrarian laws and credits, and facilitate the transportation and sale of goods.[44] It was finally concluded that the time was not ripe for the definite establishment of the Chamber of Agriculture, and the matter was remitted to the Council for decision as to future action. In the meantime, the Conference requested the convocation of a conference of agricultural specialists ; the exchange of agricultural professors and students ; the organization of museums, fairs, and popular excursions to the various countries ; the publication of a Balkan agricultural bulletin ; a conference to examine the situation of agricultural credit exhaustively and to report at the next Conference ; the Council to investigate the feasibility of an inter-Balkan Co-operative's Office.[45]

With regard to a customs union the Conference found certain prerequisites lacking. Its action, therefore, continued, as in the past, to be anticipatory.

[43] *Le Messager d'Athènes*, 18th October, 1932 ; *Les Balkans*, October-November 1932, pp. 108-111.

[44] *Le Messager d'Athènes*, 22nd October, 1932.

[45] *Les Balkans*, October-November 1932, pp. 180-181.

"The Conference invites the Council to set up a preparatory committee working in connection with the inter-Balkan
Chamber of Commerce and Industry, and with the assistance of the latter, to : (a) collect all documentation and
other data required and prepare a draft-multilateral commercial treaty to be concluded between the Balkan Countries
on the bases of : (1) a preferential inter-Balkan tariff suit-
ably applied, (2) a concerted commercial policy with a view
to protecting Balkan products in extra-Balkan markets ;
(3) to proceed, with the help of a technical sub-committee
if necessary, to carry out a detailed and comparative study
with a view to the unification of customs nomenclatures and
formalities in the Balkan States.

"The Conference recommends the inter-Balkan Chamber of Commerce and Industry to organize enquiries in
business circles as soon as possible to ascertain what are at
present the obstacles which render trade difficult or impossible.

"The Conference recommends the said Chamber to draw
up a list of articles which the Balkan countries import from
extra-Balkan countries and which could be replaced by
Balkan products, and at the same time to inform Balkan
consumers what are the products and who are the producers
of the Balkan countries and to enlighten producers as to the
requirements and tastes of consumers in the Balkan countries. For this purpose it recommends the formation of trade
museums, the publication of propaganda hand-books, the
organization of conferences, study tours and inter-Balkan
fairs in the main economic centres of the Balkans." [46]

The Communications Commission was faced with the
non-fulfillment of the resolutions of prior conferences in

[46] *Les Balkans,* October-November 1932, pp. 179-180 ; *Le Messager
d'Athènes,* 2nd November, 1932 ; League of Nations, *Bulletin of Information on the Work of International Organizations,* Vol. V, No. 1, March
1933, pp. 18-19.

its realm. It, therefore, devoted its attention largely to reconsidering the actions it had taken and to developing ways and means of securing their fulfillment. The programme developed by the Commission and approved by the Conference, called for seven things during the next year : the creation of an office in the Chamber of Commerce and Industry for the study of transportation questions ; the convocation of a conference at Athens to canvass the fulfillment of the resolutions of prior Conferences ; the inauguration of at least a part of the rail building programme ; better co-ordination of train and bus schedules ; the assembling of a civil aviation conference at Sofia in May 1933, to submit practical proposals to the next Conference for the co-ordination of this branch of communications ; the organization of a Balkan Tour, and the establishment of tourist offices and aids at the frontiers ; the establishment of a Commission on Public Works, with a conference at Sofia.[47]

The Commission on Intellectual Co-operation placed before the Conference and secured the approval of : statutes for the creation of an Institute of Balkan Historical Research ; suggestions regarding the rewriting of text-books in Balkan history and civilization ; proposals for common broadcasting programmes and film releases ; suggestions for the better dissemination of Balkan news ; and the suggestion that at the next Conference the teaching of languages, propagandist activities in schools, exchanges of school productions, and closer relations between tourist agencies be taken up.[48] In submitting the report of the Commission, Madame Cantacuzino of Rumania sagely remarked that as yet

[47] *Les Balkans, op. cit.*, pp. 190-193.
[48] *Ibid.*, pp. 194-195.

the intellectual separation between Bucharest and Sofia, and Bucharest and Istanbul was greater than that between Bucharest and Paris, in spite of the fact that among the Balkan peoples there is a certain degree of common mentality and outlook.[49] The bridging of this gulf is one of the most imperative parts of the program for ultimate federation, for political union is unthinkable without intellectual community of thought. With the subtleties of propaganda and the machinations of special interests seeking gain by selling their countries' to foreign influences, the path is a thorny and dangerous one in the Balkans. There must be a carefully preconceived, carefully executed plan ; for, if the forces of union lack plans, the forces of privilege and division are never wanting in this regard.

As a result of the labours of the Committee on Social Questions, a draft convention on the status of aliens was adopted, providing for equal rights and privileges.[50] The final article of the convention provided that it should be a part of a general Balkan pact. The question of establishing a Balkan Labour Office was adjourned until the next Conference in order to permit the gathering of more statistics and documentation concerning labour problems.[51] With respect to the traffic in women and children, the Conference requested that the governments take a greater part in the elimination of such traffic by establishing national offices for protection, adopting the League of Nations' Children's charter, developing women police officers, and by more careful examinations at the frontiers.[52] Common legislation

[49] *Les Balkans*, October-November 1932, p. 124.
[50] *Ibid.*, pp. 182-188.
[51] *Ibid.*, p. 188.
[52] *Ibid.*, pp. 188-189 ; *Le Messager d'Athènes*, 10th November, 1932.

respecting the status of married women was also urged.[53] In matters of health two sanitary conventions were advocated : one covering all of the Balkan states ; the other a special one for the Danubian states.[54] Common action against tuberculosis was also urged.[55]

v

THE speeches at the closing session of the Conference reflected, in general, a desire to close the wounds which had been opened during the meetings. Many of the speakers expressed regret over Bulgaria's action and urged her return.[56] All hailed the adoption of the pact, though several expressed more attachment to the idea and the end than they did to the pact itself.

Immediately after the close of the Conference a special Council session was held. At this all delegations, including the Bulgarians, were represented. Each of the group leaders expressed joy in the Bulgarian attendance and hope for renewed co-operation. They also pledged their efforts to see the Istanbul recommendation for bilateral conferences carried through. The Bulgarians in their turn professed a desire to co-operate and to adhere to the pact if possible.[57]

Despite the rupture caused by the Bulgarian withdrawal, the third Conference marked progress in the movement. A larger number of delegates were present, and the number of reports and documents submitted to the committees evidenced a greater amount of fore-

[53] *Les Balkans*, October-November 1932, pp. 188-189.
[54] *Ibid.*, p. 189.
[55] *Ibid.*, p. 190.
[56] *Ibid.*, pp. 160, 161, 162, 169-170.
[57] *Ibid.*, p. 171.

thought on the part of the national groups.[58]   There
was earnest co-operation among the five delegations and
a common spirit of conciliation manifest toward the
Bulgarian group.[59]   On the other hand, it must not be
overlooked that little progress had been made in enlisting the participation and support of the governments.
The Conference paid some, but not much attention to
the actual status of former resolutions, and went ahead
approving new actions without much consideration of
the possibilities of adoption by the states.   Bearing in
mind the private character of the Conference and the
broad and ultimate objectives of the movement, such
methods need not be too severely criticized.   Established political groups always lag behind the proposals
and demands of those not in power, and, to a certain
extent, depend upon them for progress.

[58] Papanastassiou, *Vers L'Union Balkanique*, p. 141, n.
[59] *Le Messager d'Athènes*, 7th November, 1932.

CHAPTER FOUR

PROGRESS RENEWED

I

THE creeping paralysis of the economic crisis, the emergence of Hitlerism in Central Europe, the weakening of the peace machinery, the atrophy of the disarmament negotiations, and the general spectre of renewed European war exerted profound influences upon the Balkans in 1933. Significant progress was made in resolving many of the differences between the states, a greater degree of official support was given to the Conference movement, and definite efforts were made to put the Conference recommendations into operation.

The centrifugal forces were strong in the Balkans. But other movements continued to draw away the attention of some states. The East European agrarian *bloc* continued its endeavour to draw into a closed circle the major grain producing states. Conferences were held but little practical advancement was made in this realm.

Various plans for a Danubian system appeared during 1933. There was, for example, the Tardieu plan, theoretically based upon Briand's idea of a European Union, but actually upon the idea of re-creating, under French influence, the economic entity which formerly existed in the old Austro-Hungarian Empire. This proposed the establishment between Austria, Czechoslovakia, Hungary, Rumania, and Yugoslavia of a preferential customs régime. Such a plan would work havoc with the idea of Balkan economic union as elaborated by the Conferences.[1] However, the realization of the Tardieu plan is remote because of the competition and conflict still existing between the Great Powers. To renascent Germany it represents but another French stratagem to be wrecked at any cost. Germany, therefore, proposes that Bulgaria be included and Czechoslovakia excluded, paving the way for the re-establishment of German domination in Central and Eastern Europe and the suffocation of Czechoslovakia, the chief pivot of French power. To Italy it would mean French victory and Italian defeat in the game of influence and loans in Central Europe with the consequent gradual decline of Trieste and Fiume as profitable transfer ports. To Czechoslovakia and the Little Entente, adoption of the Tardieu plan would mean a victory for their policy of economic collaboration by Austria and Hungary before settling the political and territorial issues. To Hungary it would mean sacrificing the opposite policy, consistently followed since 1920.

Another suggestion, the application of which would have a bearing upon the Balkan movement, came from Turkey during the year. She proposed a Black Sea Pact for the neutralization of the Black Sea and the Straits. Russia, Rumania, Bulgaria, Greece, and Turkey were to be the members.[2] While such an arrangement as this would not run counter to the Balkan union, and while the neutralization of dangerous zones is a highly desirable thing, the same end could be achieved by a pact between Russia on the one hand and the

[1] Papanastassiou, *op. cit.*, p. 162.
[2] *Ibid.*, p. 163.

Balkan group as a unit on the other. Such a plan would further the movement toward union rather than distract attention from it.

But the combination having the greatest significance for the Balkan movement was the Little Entente. In February, 1933, the world was notified of the adoption of the Pact of Permanent Organization of the Little Entente.[3] By Article 6 of this pact it was required that every political treaty, unilateral act, and economic accord between a member of the Little Entente and a third party must have, in order to be valid, the unanimous consent of the Council of the Little Entente.[4] This created misgivings. It was feared that this signified a definite orientation of Rumania and Yugoslavia away from the Balkans, and that it was either a covering by means of which they were diplomatically seeking withdrawal, or that it was a renewed extension of Czechoslovakian and French power into Eastern Europe. However, at the Balkan Council meeting in March these doubts "were entirely removed by the assurances of the delegations of the two countries." M. Titulescu told M. Papanastassiou that the pact in no way conflicted with the Balkan grouping, and added that he was proud Rumania belonged to the Balkan peoples.[5] Similar assurances were subsequently given to representatives of the other Balkan states by Titulescu, who at that time was President of the Little Entente Council.[6]

Political relations between these two groups are prob-

[3] *American Journal of International Law, Official Documents,* July 1933, p. 117 ff.

[4] E. Benes, *Le Pacte d'Organization de la Petite Entente,* Prague, 1933.

[5] *The Near East and India,* 30th March, 1933, p. 241; Papanastassiou, *op. cit.,* p. 158.

[6] Papanastassiou, *op. cit.,* p. 158.

ably less likely to lead to complications than are the economic relations. There are no important political differences between them. Both aim at conserving the peace and it is entirely possible for them to become supplementary to each other in this effort. In fact, with two of the Balkan countries in the Little Entente, the latter may perform a very useful function in uniting and mediating between the western and eastern sections of Europe. The difficulties which both face come from elsewhere, to wit, the differences between France, Germany, and Italy.[7] Close relations between the Little Entente and the Balkans ought to mean strength for peace.

But economic relations are more complex. There is definite economic competition at present ; and, if the Little Entente carries out its programme of economic accord, special tariff measures and agreements will be necessary. Efforts have been made by the Little Entente to develop economic union[8] but little tangible progress has resulted thus far.[9] If either group should succeed in organizing an economic union, the conclusion of a new convention to govern the relations between the two *blocs* may become necessary and advisable.

II

THE Balkan Council met in Bucharest the 17th-20th March, 1933. The tardiness of the session was due less to the influence of these extra-Balkan movements than to the political disturbances in Rumania, and difficulties

---

[7] Papanastassiou, *op. cit.*, p. 153.

[8] J. O. Crane, *The Little Entente*, New York, 1931, Chap. XI ; F. Codrescu, *La Petite Entente*, Paris, 1933, Chap. XI.

[9] *Central European Observer*, 12th January, 1934 ; *ibid.*, 26th January, 1934.

within the membership of one or two of the national groups.[10] All groups were represented and a new spirit of friendliness and accord was manifest.

The most important action taken by the Council was the unanimous adoption of a resolution requesting each delegation to urge upon its government the acceptance and execution of the Conference recommendations and resolutions.[11] This naturally embraced the draft pact adopted at Bucharest. The favourable vote of the Bulgarians indicated a new policy on their part.[12] To speed the progress of the movement, it was also voted that a commission should be formed to visit each country to hold public meetings.

In line with the same idea, but marking somewhat of a departure from the original theory of the movement, it was voted on the recommendation of the Greek representative that the Conference resolutions come into force if two or more states adopted them.[13] This served to legalize the postal union drawn up by the Conference in 1931 and ratified by Greece and Turkey. It also paved the way for the application of the draft pact should Bulgaria desire to withhold her signature, and would prevent any "loss of face" which might come to her by such action. The adoption of such a device, while perhaps serving to start wheels moving, is a dangerous tactic — as the experience in the League of Nations has frequently demonstrated — for it weakens the sense of collective responsibility, renders shelving easy, and may provoke cliques and combinations.

The agenda for the next Conference was drawn up,

[10] *Les Balkans*, March-April 1933, p. 545.
[11] *Ibid*, p. 547.
[12] Papanastassiou, *op. cit.*, p. 167.
[13] *Les Balkans*, March-April 1933, p. 548.

and the Council adjourned after having decided to meet at Salonika instead of at Belgrade. This was done out of deference to the Bulgarians who did not wish to go to Belgrade until the frontier and minority issues were more amicably composed.

During the Council meetings a telegram was received from Geneva announcing the first gathering of the ministers of the Balkan states, in conformity with the recommendations of the Conferences.[14] The meeting in Geneva took the form of mutual personal and national felicitations. Nothing constructive was accomplished, and none of the Conference actions were considered. However, diplomacy always requires the display of more pomp and circumstance than unofficial action, and the diplomats may be pardoned these first gestures of etiquette if in subsequent gatherings serious matters are entertained.

Immediately after the Council sessions a series of bilateral conferences took place. The first was held by the Bulgarians and Yugoslavians before quitting Bucharest. Although it was held in an amicable mood, no accord resulted. The other conferences were more successful. The Bulgar-Turk and Bulgar-Greek conferences at Sofia resulted in the issuance of "protocols" by which the three national groups agreed to work together for *rapprochement,* and for putting into effect in their countries the Conference recommendations.[15]

---

[14] *Les Balkans,* March-April 1933, p. 546.
[15] Papanastassiou, *op. cit.,* pp. 167-168 ; See also *Les Balkans,* March-April 1933, p. 550.

III

THE interval between the meeting of the Council and the Conference witnessed three significant developments : (1) a large number of Balkan gatherings ; (2) the conclusion of a series of important treaties ; (3) the development of an epidemic of royal and ministerial visitations.

Meetings in the nature of sub-commissions [16] were held in every capital. "International gatherings among the Balkan peoples," noted one paper, "have become to such an extent the order of the day that capacity to give itself a Balkan international setting is accepted as the hall-mark of the national status of a public body in any realm." [17] A maritime conference was held at Athens. Conferences of journalists, officials of municipalities, and on the agrarian question were held at Bucharest. In Sofia a highly significant meeting of representatives of the Orthodox Churches of Bulgaria and Yugoslavia was held, as well as inter-Balkan gatherings on communications, travel, and public works. At Belgrade a medical conference met. And at Istanbul tobacco, industrial, and merchants' conferences were held, at the first of which Bulgaria, Greece, and Turkey concluded a treaty for the common protection of the oriental tobacco trade.[18] Without in any way minimizing the work or importance of any of these, perhaps the most valuable action from the point of view of future solidarity was the formation both in Bulgaria and Yugo-

---

[16] Papanastassiou, *op. cit.*, p. 168.

[17] *The Near East and India,* 11th March, 1933, p. 371.

[18] *Les Balkans,* March-April 1933, p. 550 ; *ibid.,* September-October 1933, pp. 667-668 ; Papanastassiou, *op. cit.,* p. 170 ; *The Near East and India,* 28th September, 1933, p. 798.

slavia of Bulgar-Yugoslav Societies. These were
founded for the purpose of forwarding good will and
met with favourable response in both nations. Lectures, exhibits, and libraries were established in various
centres, and at once became influential nucleii.[19]

Events in Western Europe were largely responsible
for the second important development in 1933. The
increasingly belligerent and sinister power of Hitlerism,
the advocacy and promotion of the Italian Four Power
Pact, the dissipation of the disarmament program, all
pointed to a return to pre-war diplomacy. While there
can be little doubt in the mind of a non-European that
the 1919-1920 peace terms juggled the small racial
groups of Europe for the purpose of redressing the
balance of power, and while there can likewise be little
doubt to a foreigner that the Central and Eastern European states have been very cleverly and masterfully
manipulated by France, within and without the League
of Nations in the years since 1919, nevertheless, an
outright return to the pre-war and pre-League system
with two competitive, armed, hostile, and determined
groups in Western Europe would lead in the near future
to the old intrigue, sacrifice, and destruction of the
small Central and Eastern states. All, save perhaps
Hungary, which has been so emasculated already as to
preclude any further damage, are determined to prevent
a return to such an infernal world.

One of the major problems in the Eastern situation
since the war has been the policy of Soviet Russia.
The cries of some radicals for world revolution, and the
sullen attitude on the Bessarabian question have bred

[19] *The Near East and India*, 9th November, 1933, p. 926 ; *Les Balkans*,
September-October 1933, pp. 666-667.

much uneasiness. All has not been one-sided, however, for the Soviets have been uneasy over what Poland and Rumania might do in case of war in the Far East. Such mutual feelings paved the way for reconciliation when, in 1933, threats to peace materialized in Europe and in Asia. But, the two Conventions Defining Aggression, drawn up at London in June (one between Soviet Russia and Afghanistan, Estonia, Latvia, Persia, Poland, Rumania, and Turkey ; the other between Soviet Russia and Czechoslovakia, Rumania, Turkey, and Yugoslavia),[20] not only opened the door to amicable understanding in the Near East, and defined "aggression" with greater precision than any other compact, but also threw the Bulgarian situation into sharp relief. Bulgaria was isolated more than ever from the Slav world, assuming that disinterested Slav solidarity has ever existed ! And the finger of accusation was seen pointing unmistakably at her in Article 2, which declared to be an aggressor a state giving "aid to armed bands formed on the territory of a State and invading the territory of another State ; or refusal, despite demands on the part of the State subjected to attack, to take all possible measures on its own territory to deprive the said bands of any aid and protection." [21]   The Sofia correspondent of *The Near East and India* reported that Bulgaria was "thrown into a panic" by these Conventions.[22]   The Conventions removed the most serious cause for worry in the Near East[23] — the policy of Soviet Russia —, and, as subsequent events have demon-

---

[20] *American Journal of International Law, Official Documents,* October 1933, p. 192 *et seq.*
[21] *Ibid.,* p. 193.
[22] Issue of 10th August, 1933, p. 649.
[23] *L'Europe Nouvelle,* 14th October, 1933, pp. 988-991.

strated, they were instrumental in producing a radical change in Bulgarian administration and foreign policy calculated to bring that country again within the fold of organized Slavdom and Balkan union.

More localized in application, but of almost equal significance and influence, was the Græco-Turkish Pact of Entente Cordiale drawn up at Ankara the 14th September, 1933. According to this treaty, both states : mutually guarantee the integrity and *status quo* of their common frontier — Thrace ; agree that in all international questions of interest to them to hold a preliminary consultation ; declare themselves ready to consider that in all international meetings involving limited representation the delegate of either of them will have power to act for their common, as well as for their particular interests ; and that in such events, to entrust the representation to the one whose interests appear to be predominant.[24]

This agreement was spoken of as a foundation, and as a nucleus for a Balkan federation,[25] although it is a closed treaty. Ismet Pasha is reported to have said, "Ententes between two countries can gradually be transformed into regional agreements, which, given good-will, should result sooner or later in a general agreement, which international conferences have failed to bring about." [26]

Bulgarian opinion, "thrown into a panic" by the London conventions, now saw in this treaty an end for the cherished hope of a territorial outlet on the Ægean Sea.[27] Bulgaria was again being made to feel the out-

[24] Text in *L'Europe Nouvelle*, 14th October, 1933, p. 996.
[25] Papanastassiou, *op. cit.*, p. 165.
[26] *The Near East and India*, 21st September, 1933, p. 773.
[27] Papanastassiou, *op. cit.*, p. 166.

cast's position.   However, Rushtu Bey, visiting Sofia a
few weeks later, assured her that Turkey would be glad
to conclude a similar pact with her and urged the initiation of steps toward that end.[28]   As an intermediate
step, the two states renewed their existing convention
of amity and pacific settlement.[29]   Greece also took
action to show a friendly attitude.   She assured Bulgaria of her continued readiness to discuss the provision of preferential opportunities in an Ægean port
and on connecting railroads.[30]   And she went further
by re-establishing commercial relations with Bulgaria,
and by instituting a Græco-Bulgarian Mixed Commission to settle outstanding commercial differences.[31]

The principles, and some of the phraseology, of the
draft Balkan pact were adopted and put into force during the autumn months by Rumania, Russia, Turkey,
and Yugoslavia in a series of Conventions of Friendship
and Peaceful Settlement of Disputes.[32]   In line with
the meeting of the foreign ministers earlier in the year,
this marked another advance and victory for the movement set on foot by the Conferences.

In September the Greek Chamber of Deputies de-
bated the Balkan movement, and, after a favourable
discussion, ordered its president to communicate with
the presidents of the other Balkan chambers, urging
upon their governments interest and support.[33]   Re-

[28] *The Near East and India*, 9th November, 1933, p. 927 ; *L'Europe
Nouvelle*, 16th December, 1933, p. 1207.

[29] Papanastassiou, *op. cit.*, p. 166.

[30] *Ibid.*

[31] *Ibid.*; *Les Balkans*, September-October 1933, p. 587.

[32] *Ibid.* ; *The Near East and India*, 26th October, 1933, pp. 873-874 ;
ibid., 16th November, 1933, pp. 946-947.

[33] *Les Balkans*, September-October 1933, pp. 661-662 ; *The Near East
and India*, 21st September, 1933, p. 773.

sponses were made by all the other chambers, although their replies were couched in such broad, vague, and meaningless phraseology as to indicate more by way of lip service than genuine conviction for the movement.[34] Following this but perhaps not in any way connected with it, a new series of royal and ministerial visitations began.[35] M. Titulescu, Foreign Minister of Rumania and President of the Council of the Little Entente, inaugurated the series, visiting Sofia, Belgrade, and Ankara in October 1933. King Alexander of Yugoslavia followed, visiting the rulers of Bulgaria (at Varna), Rumania, Turkey, and Greece. King Boris of Bulgaria conferred with Carol of Rumania on the Danube and subsequently at Sinaia. He also conferred twice with Alexander in Yugoslavian territory, on his way to and from the funeral of King Albert of Belgium. On both occasions, his passage through Yugoslavian territory was marked by friendly demonstrations.

It is questionable whether the chief objective of these and later visitations [36] was the affirmation of the Balkan interests of all of the states. It will be noted that the visits were led by representatives of the Little Entente states. These states were faced with several serious problems including the spread of Germanic National Socialism, and increased propaganda for Hungarian revision, and one wonders whether much of the diplomatic itineration was not designed to draw Bulgaria into the orbit of the Little Entente. In addition, of course, any agreement which might evolve to guarantee

[34] *Les Balkans*, September-October 1933, pp. 663-665.
[35] *Foreign Policy Reports*, New York, 9th May, 1934, p. 62.
[36] See *New York Times*, 28th September, 1934, for report of favourable visit of Alexander to Boris at Sofia.

the Balkan *status quo* in the event of war to the west would be extremely valuable. Whatever may have been the ulterior motives behind these interviews, the indication which they were intended to convey was that high official circles were interested in improving international relations. Subsequent correspondence from the Balkans spoke of the creation of a new spirit.[37] Between Bulgaria and Yugoslavia "a radical change" was said to have taken place.[38]

IV

CLARIFICATION of motives and proof of changed attitudes waited upon subsequent developments, not the least of which was the fourth Conference. This Conference was scheduled to meet in Salonika in September, but was postponed until November. Various reasons were offered by those in favour of postponement, such as conflict with the sessions of the League of Nations, the Inter-Parliamentary Conference, and the desire for time to permit the governments to carry through their programmes of negotiation.[39] Fortunately the Conference meetings were successful enough to dispel impressions of weakening.

The Council held a meeting the day before the Conference assembled. At this meeting all groups were represented. It was decided not to favour the creation of any more new institutions until those already voted were functioning satisfactorily.[40] A disturbance threatened when the Yugoslavian delegate urged that

---

[37] *L'Europe Nouvelle*, 14th October, 1933, p. 990 ; *ibid.*, 16th December, 1933, p. 1194.

[38] *The Near East and India*, 28th September, 1933, p. 796.

[39] Papanastassiou, *op. cit.*, p. 176.

[40] *Les Balkans*, November-December 1933, p. 993.

the Conference avoid reopening specific measures respecting the minorities. This was not with the idea of avoiding the issue, but in order that this Conference might be spared the dissensions of the previous ones, and that there might be emphasis upon agreements rather than disagreements. However, the Bulgarian representative contented himself with endorsing the idea of concord, and the declaration received the consent of all.[41]

The agenda for the fourth Conference included the following matters :

I. Commission on Organization of the Conference.
   (1) Modification of the statute of the Conference.
   (2) Model statute for national groups.

II. Political Commission.
   (1) Application of resolutions of preceding conferences, including those respecting minorities.
   (2) Unification of consular conventions.

III. Commission on Intellectual *Rapprochement*.
   (1) Language study in each country.
   (2) Study-week consecrated to Balkan countries.
   (3) Creation of a sub-committee for co-operation of physical education and sport organizations.

IV. Economics Commission.
   (1) Project for economic co-operation.
   (2) Statute for Maritime section of Chamber of Commerce and Industry.
   (3) Agricultural questions :
      a. Credit.
      b. Balkan Agriculture and international trade.
      c. Chambers of agriculture.

[41] *Les Balkans,* November-December 1933, p. 993 ; Papanastassiou, *op. cit.,* p. 180.

d. Projects for Balkan office of Co-operatives.

V. Communications.
  (1) Development of civil aviation services.
  (2) Air routes.
  (3) Revision and co-ordination of resolutions of previous Conferences.
  (4) Execution of resolutions concerning foreign travel.

VI. Social Policy and Health.
  (1) Statutes of Balkan Labour Office.
  (2) Sanitary and veterinary conventions.
  (3) Protection of women in industry.
  (4) Rural hygiene.[42]

The first session of the Conference was held at the University of Salonika, with the largest number of delegates of any of the Conferences. All states had diplomatic representatives at the meeting, and the delegations included many persons of high official standing. In his presidential address, M. Papanastassiou pointed out that while the breakdown in international co-operation was evident in the League of Nations, progress was apparent in the Balkans, although many of the resolutions of earlier Conferences had not been carried out.[43] The struggle for union was not so much against the forces of nature, he asserted, as against the will of men. M. Natchi, leader of the Albanian group, observed that while the draft Balkan pact looked good, no one took steps to secure its adoption by the governments. He chided Greece and Turkey on their new agreement, say-

---

[42] *Les Balkans*, March-April 1933, pp. 549-550.
[43] *Les Balkans*, November-December 1933, pp. 996-999.

ing that it offered nothing to the group as a whole, but was a regional defence and stability convention, whereas what the Balkans needed was something which would make a *bloc* of all the states.[44] This was answered by Hassan Bey, representing Turkey, who said that such bilateral pacts were made to avoid intrigue and misunderstanding, and were thus in reality steps toward union.[45] M. Sakizov, head of the Bulgarian delegation, said that if questions involving difficulties were raised, it was with a purpose of sincerely trying to find honest solutions. He concluded his speech pleading for patience in the face of great problems, thus displaying a somewhat different attitude from that shown at Bucharest the year before.[46] M. Yovanovitch of Yugoslavia gave expression to practically the same view.[47]

From these and the other speeches at the first plenary session, it was apparent that this Conference was opening with the delegations taking more conciliatory views than in 1932. The adoption of this attitude, however, did not preclude frankness and realism.

Although the atmosphere was considerably clearer, the work of the Political Commission was still charged with dangerous possibilities. While examining the efficacy of past recommendations, the Bulgarians proposed that there be bilateral meetings of the foreign ministers instead of general annual gatherings, as requested. They also suggested that definite topics be proposed for the ministers to discuss.[48] Other delegates saw in these proposals reversion to the old Bulgarian thesis,

[44] *Les Balkans*, November-December 1933, p. 1004.
[45] *Ibid.*, p. 1009.
[46] *Ibid.*, p. 1005.
[47] *Ibid.*, p. 1010.
[48] *Ibid.*, p. 1015 ; Papanastassiou, *op. cit.*, p. 183.

and strongly combated them.[49]   M. Pella of Rumania, however, sought to compromise the evanescent conflict, and advanced a proposal incorporating both ideas : the general conference of ministers, and bilateral interviews for the solution of particular troubles.   This sane proposal was accepted by all.[50]

Trouble threatened again when the Political Commission undertook the consideration of an appeal to the governments to consider the adoption of the draft pact. The Bulgarians entered the argument that the pact did not accord them equality with the others, and, that while Bulgaria was in favour of the pact it could not adopt it until such equality was recognized, loyal application of the minorities treaties was assured, and amendments made to Chapter Four to render the protection more efficacious.[51]   Mm. Papanastassiou and Pella opposed this new Bulgarian contention, arguing that the Conference work was private, that the governments were free to make any changes in the pact, and that the essential thing to do in the Conference was to get all of the delegations lined up behind the idea of a Balkan pact.   The Bulgarians replied that they did not consider it absolutely essential that agreement on disputed questions be reached before a treaty be concluded, but that they receive at least a "commencement of satisfaction."[52]   Further controversy ensued when the Rumanians, Turks, and Yugoslavs answered by emphasizing the need of amending the pact to define with exactitude an "aggressor,"[53] preferably along the lines

[49] Papanastassiou, *op. cit.*, p. 183.
[50] *Les Balkans, supra,* p. 1017 ; Papanastassiou, *op. cit.*, p. 182.
[51] *Les Balkans, supra,* p. 1018 ; Papanastassiou, *op. cit.*, p. 183.
[52] *Affaires Etrangères*, Paris, December 1933, p. 615.
[53] *Ibid.*, pp. 615-616.

of the London Conventions. To prevent spread of the controversy, the Greeks then called attention to the fact that the agenda did not call for a discussion of the pact, only of a recommendation urging the adoption of it as approved at Bucharest.[54]

With matters again heading for the old battlefield, the entire issue was taken away from the Commission to a special session of the Council. After lengthy debate, the Bulgarian propositions were rejected *in toto,* and in their place a Rumanian compromise was suggested, at the voting of which by the Assembly the Bulgarians were to be permitted to state their case.[55] The compromise unanimously adopted at the third plenary session, stated that :

"The Conference, recognizing the great interest which prompts the drafting of a multilateral Pact between the six Balkan States

"Renews the resolution of the Third Conference concerning the Balkan Pact, requesting the respective governments to conclude a multilateral Pact on the basis of the principles contained in the draft Pact adopted by the Third Conference

"It expresses also the wish that the governments modify the provisions of the Pact to conform to circumstantial differences and to the progress which may be made in this realm." [56]

After the Commission's report was unanimously adopted, the Bulgarian group made a declaration accepting the pact, on the ground that the equality of Bulgaria be accepted, that the minorities provisions be

---

[54] *Affaires Etrangères,* Paris, December 1933, p. 616 ; *Les Balkans, supra,* pp. 1019-1021.

[55] *Les Balkans, supra,* pp. 1020-1021.

[56] *Ibid.,* pp. 1087-1088 ; Papanastassiou, *op. cit.,* p. 187.

loyally carried out, and that the Conference aid in sur-
mounting the special problems facing the Bulgarians.
The Yugoslavian delegation played a new rôle, keeping silent and refraining from precipitating strife by
refutation. The other delegations saluted the new
positions.[57]   Thus, while the fourth Conference did not
go beyond the third in promoting new political devices, it was able to unite all groups behind the idea of
the draft pact, and to make some headway in resolving
the most ticklish issue in the Balkans.[58]   The compromise resolution offered by the Rumanians was not only
an admirable device for averting a deadlock, but offered
a happy means by which the Balkan states could avail
themselves, as they saw fit, of the provisions contained
in the draft pact. The conclusion of the Balkan
Entente, and the ratification of the Argentine Anti-
War Pact during 1934 may be said to be the governments' answer to the Rumanian suggestion.

v

In considering the statute of the Conference two points
of view developed. The Greek delegation sponsored a
revision which would convert the movement into a
parliamentary gathering, with the majority of the delegates members of parliaments.[59]   The Yugoslavian
group, on the other hand, sought to amend the statute
to make the Conference entirely private, excluding all
persons in governmental or political service. After

[57] *Les Balkans, supra*, pp. 1055-1059 ; Papanastassiou, *op. cit.*, p. 188.

[58] A pamphlet issued by the Bulgarian National Group, after the Confer-
ence, entitled *Bulgaria and the Balkan Problems* (Sofia, 1934), stated that
"We are deeply convinced that the worst Peace is preferable to the most
Glorious War." p. 7.

[59] Papanastassiou, *op. cit.*, pp. 217-218.

long debate it was decided to refer the matter to the Council and to the next Conference for further consideration, although most of the representatives appeared to favour the Greek rather than the Yugoslav proposal.

One of the most important items before the Economic Commission was that of a proposal for economic union, submitted by the Greek national group, and intended to implement the political pact of union. The draft as submitted by the Greeks was widely amended,[60] but unanimously adopted by the Conference.[61]

This proposal showed considerably more advanced thought and less partisan animosity than the political pact. According to the preamble, the purpose was to develop to the greatest possible degree the exchange of products and services among the Balkan states, and to secure the maximum protection for the principal Balkan goods in extra-Balkan markets.

As means of realizing these ends, the draft suggested : special "most-favoured-nation" treatment for Balkan goods through new treaties, insertions of special Balkan exemption clauses in other commercial treaties, lowest tariff rates ; a common commercial policy for the export of Balkan goods and sales in foreign markets ; the creation of a Compensation Chamber to facilitate transactions in credits, exchange, and transfer ; the creation of a Permanent Commerce Commission to encourage commerce, co-ordinate policies, advise methods of eliminating duplication and conflict, and propose new commercial agreements. This Permanent Commission is to differ from the Chamber of Commerce and In-

[60] Papanastassiou, *op. cit.*, p. 199.
[61] *Ibid.*, pp. 263-268 ; *Les Balkans, supra*, pp. 1088-1091.

dustry set up at Istanbul by being a public or state-controlled organ. If carried through, this "regional economic entente" will mark a major step toward the ultimate union of the Balkan states.

Extensive consideration was also given to the other major economic problem, the agricultural situation. Consideration was given to a Balkan Co-operatives' Office, which was approved.[62] This organization, private in nature, was to unify the work of the co-operative movements, lend weight to their efforts for favourable legislation, and facilitate by all possible means the evolution of an agricultural agreement among the various countries.[63] The other practical step related to the question of agricultural credit. The Conference, having in mind an unfulfilled resolution of the third Conference, requested the Yugoslavian group to make an exhaustive study of the matter, call a special meeting of experts and bankers at Belgrade, and submit suggestions for action.[64] It was also agreed that the states ought to favour co-operative societies ; that Central Co-operative Unions ought to be founded in each ; that short-term agricultural credits ought to be organized by co-operative groups ; that most favourable trade treatment should be given in each state to the agricultural products of the other Balkan states ; that agricultural banks should be prepared to give credit outside of their countries ; that agricultural goods coming from extra-Balkan states ought to be revalorized in order to give greater benefits to Balkan products and in order to present a common tariff barrier ; and that

[62] *Les Balkans, supra,* pp. 1091-1093.
[63] Article 2.
[64] *Les Balkans, supra,* p. 1094.

treaties of commerce be concluded at once among states not having them.[65]

While the Conferences have thus far been able to do relatively little by way of practical relief for agriculture, they have demonstrated the possibilities of action if the states could be persuaded to accept their proposals. Co-ordination and combination can be the only hope of Balkan agriculture, and the Conferences have at least performed the public service of sketching possible methods.

The Commission on Intellectual Reconciliation confined its attention to matters which had already been discussed previously, hoping thereby to concentrate upon the achievement of a few objectives. Courses on Balkan languages and literature in Balkan universities were again favoured, along with the establishment of chairs of History of Balkan Civilization, and inauguration of Balkan Weeks in the universities and schools, where, significantly enough, little had been done to forward peace and federation. Finally, responsibility was placed upon the national groups to report each year what steps they had taken to carry out the resolutions and actions of the Conference.[66]

In the realm of communications and travel, the Conference was faced with the identical situation prevailing the year before. None of the recommendations had been translated into official action, with the exception of Yugoslavian adherence to the Balkan Postal Union, which was hailed with much enthusiasm. By way of pragmatic work, the Conference approved the statute for the Maritime Section of the Chamber of Commerce

[65] *Les Balkans, supra,* p. 1093.
[66] *Ibid.,* pp. 1094-1095.

and Industry.[67]   This office was charged with a host of
activities designed to foster, protect, and aid maritime
trade and transportation. If the labours of this organization meet with any success, considerable improvement
in communications and in the shipping business should
result.   But, it must not be overlooked that the maritime office is purely private and its suggestions lack
force, either with business men or with governments.

While many of its former recommendations had not
been put into effect, the Commission returned to the
charge, urging (1) the construction of direct rail routes
between Salonika-Sofia-Bucharest, and between Albania,
Greece, and Yugoslavia ; (2) the revision of schedules
for better connections and through cars between all important cities ; (3) the revision of rates within the
peninsula ; (4) the construction or completion of trunk-
highways between the several states ; (5) the reduction
of forbidden flying zones ; (6) the application of the
1919 aërial convention ; (7) common protection for
civil airways and recognition of equality of rights of
civil aircraft ; (8) relaxation of frontier examinations and
visas; (9) creation of combined customs and police posts
at frontiers; (10) the convocation of a technical commission on transportation before the next Conference.[68]
The questions of a concerted public works programme,
and the regulations for an aëronautical office were
ordered placed on the agenda for the next Conference.

The Committee on Social Policies approved the draft
of a convention for a Balkan Labour Office modeled
after the International Labour Office.[69]   The office, if

[67] *Les Balkans, supra*, pp. 1097-1099.
[68] *Ibid.*, pp. 1095-1100.
[69] *Ibid.*, pp. 1100-1102.

established by the states, is to be directly related to the Geneva body, and is to perform the same functions ; to wit : the centralization and publication of labour information, the preparation of conventions, and the study of all questions affecting labour.[70]   In addition, the resolutions of the Commission requested active sanitary and veterinary co-operation,[71] the inauguration of social insurance for women and children in labour, equal rights of work and equal minimum wages for men and women, and the inclusion of women in national delegations to the Balkan Conferences.[72]

VI

At the final session of the Conference the common note was one of optimism.   M. Papanastassiou said that the Conference dispelled all of the fears held before its convocation, and that from the points of view of the numbers and standings of the delegates, the interest of the press and the governments, and the spirit of accord and constructive statesmanship, the Salonika Conference marked a new high-water mark for the movement.[73] M. Sakizov of the Bulgarian group added further hope, by saying that this Conference had been the most fruitful of all, and that in this new spirit a solution could be found for all problems.   In fine, the spirit at adjournment was captured by Rushtu Eschref Bey when he cried, *"En avant et pleins d'espérance."* [74]

[70] Chapter I.
[71] *Les Balkans, supra,* p. 1103.
[72] *Ibid,* p. 1104.
[73] *Ibid.,* pp. 1072-1074.
[74] *Les Balkans, supra,* p. 1081.

CHAPTER FIVE

THE BALKAN ENTENTE

DIPLOMACY'S FIRST MOVE TOWARD UNITY

I

THE unprecedented diplomatic activity which had taken place before the fourth Conference resumed its course shortly afterward. Turkish and Albanian ministers visited Belgrade. As a result of the negotiations, trade agreements were reached, and Turkey and Yugoslavia concluded a new treaty of friendship and non-aggression.[1] This was similar to the other treaties of the same type which had been concluded by the two states with other parties in recent years. King Boris of Bulgaria subsequently visited Yugoslavia and Rumania. His visit to Yugoslavia was followed by that of the Greek Foreign Minister. It was widely rumoured that a Balkan pact was under consideration, although on the 26th November, 1933, Foreign Minister Rushtu Bey of Turkey denied that the signature of such a pact was imminent.[2] However, few doubted that the numerous conversations were prompted by a desire to find safeguards for Balkan security in the event that developments in the west took a turn for the worse.

The real purpose of the negotiations was revealed, and

[1] *London Times*, 29th November, p. 13.
[2] *Ibid.*, 27th November, 1933, p. 13.

rumours substantiated, by the signature of an important "Balkan Pact" at Athens on the 9th February, 1934, Greece, Rumania, Turkey, and Yugoslavia being the signatories. Unfortunately Albania was not invited to sign, and the signatories would not draft a treaty which would meet with Bulgarian suggestions. The failure to invite Albania was explained as an effort to avoid giving offence to Italy, who had been charged with the protection of Albania by a declaration of the Allies to the League of Nations, and substantiated by the Council ; [3] an agreement which Albania announced she had never recognized, and, so far as she was concerned, did not exist. [4]

The absence of Bulgaria from the list of signatories must be explained on very different grounds. Bulgaria was not ignored. Indeed much of the negotiation had revolved about her. When in Sofia in October, it appears that M. Tsaldaris, the Greek Foreign Minister, had invited M. Mouchanov, the Bulgarian Prime Minister, to draft the text of a Balkan Pact. M. Mouchanov proposed that a pact of non-aggression within the framework of the League of Nations and in the spirit of the Kellogg Pact was the most appropriate way to reaffirm peace between the Balkan peoples. The plan was not acceptable to Tsaldaris, and, in his rejection was revealed the real purpose which the signatories hoped to achieve by a Balkan Pact. He informed Mouchanov that it must contain a guarantee of the territorial *status quo,* and a renunciation of treaty revision. [5] Such an agreement would involve a complete abdication of the

---

[3] Papanastassiou, *op. cit.*, p. 226.
[4] *The Near East and India*, 10th May, 1934, p. 354.
[5] *Ibid.*, 22nd February, 1934, p. 144.

policy followed by all Bulgarian statesmen. Mouchanov informed Tsaldaris, and subsequently the
Rumanians, that Bulgaria would be glad to conclude
bilateral security pacts with each of the Balkan states.
He explained, "We have given proofs that we never
have had the intention nor the desire of modifying by
violence the frontiers established by the treaties," [6] but
"the Bulgarian people cannot ... renounce rights guaranteed to them by the League of Nations." [7] Bilateral
pacts were not regarded as adequate substitutes by
either the Greeks or the Rumanians, any more than they
had been by the Conferences, and the four states
thereupon hastened to the conclusion of the multi-
lateral Pact without further consultation with Bulgaria.
Nevertheless, it appears that assurances were given to
Bulgaria that the Pact would not be directed at her
and that the signatories would subsequently be willing
to conclude bilateral pacts with her as suggested by
Mouchanov.[8]

On February 1st Premier Mouchanov appeared before
the Bulgarian Foreign Affairs Commission and publicly
announced that Bulgaria could not be a party to a
Balkan Pact guaranteeing the *status quo* of the present
frontiers. He renewed the offer of concluding non-
aggression treaties providing guarantees of Balkan
peace.[9] A manifesto was issued by the Internal Macedonian Revolutionary Organization declaring a recess
on frontier incidents and welcoming a Balkan Pact if
the latter would guarantee the political and cultural

[6] *Les Balkans*, January-February 1934, p. 106.

[7] *The Near East and India*, 22nd February, 1934, p. 144.

[8] Papanastassiou, *op. cit.*, p. 232 ; *The Near East and India*, 22nd February, 1934, p. 144.

[9] *New York Times*, 2nd February, 1934.

rights of the Macedonian minorities in Yugoslavia and Greece.[10]

The terms of the Balkan Pact are few and concise :

"The President of the Republic of Greece,
His Majesty the King of Rumania,
The President of the Republic of Turkey,
His Majesty the King of Yugoslavia,

United in the desire to contribute toward the permanence of peace in the Balkans, animated by the spirit of mutual understanding and of conciliation which inspired the development of the Pact of Paris and the decisions relative thereto by the Assembly of the League of Nations, firmly determined to assure respect for contractual agreements already existing and the maintenance of present territorial boundaries in the Balkans, have decided to conclude a Balkan Pact, and to that effect have designated as their respective plenipotentiaries : . . .

Article I. Greece, Rumania, Turkey, and Yugoslavia mutually guarantee the security of all their Balkan frontiers.

Article II. The high contracting parties obligate themselves to agree upon measures to be taken in case of eventualities capable of affecting their interests as defined in this agreement. They pledge themselves not to undertake any political action as regards any other Balkan country not a signatory to the present agreement without previous mutual conference and not to assume any political obligation toward any other Balkan country without the consent of the other contracting parties.

Article III. This agreement will enter into full force and effect from the time of its signature by all the contracting powers and will be ratified as speedily as possible. It will be open to all Balkan countries, whose adhesion will be

[10] *New York Times*, 21st January, 1934, p. 2E.

favorably looked upon by the contracting parties, and will take effect when the other signatory countries shall have expressed their agreement.

"In witness whereof . . ." [11]

After initialling the Pact, the ministers held a meeting which was announced as that of *"Le Conseil de l'Entente Balkanique."* Means of developing political, economic, and juridical relations were discussed. An announcement indicated that the ministers intended to meet regularly after the fashion of the Little Entente ministers.[12] At an official dinner which was tendered to the plenipotentiaries, several revealed a bit of the spirit behind the Pact, and strangely betrayed not a little apprehension over its general acceptability. M. Maximos, recognized as the originator of the instrument, sought to apprehend criticism from the Balkan Conference by asserting that while they had not realized in their totality the aspirations of the "apostles of the Balkan idea," they were nevertheless motivated by "this vast movement of ideas," and had achieved all that the exigencies of the time would permit.[13] Sensing opposition likely to arise as a result of the absence of Bulgaria and the emphasis upon the preservation of the *status quo,* Mm. Maximos and Titulescu both denied that the Pact was directed at anyone,[14] although M. Titulescu proceeded to emphasize that the fundamental desire was to provide security against "that reaction" commenced in Central Europe, but continuing and rising today in

[11] *New York Times,* 18th March, 1934 ; *L'Europe Nouvelle,* 17th February, 1934, p. 173 ; Papanastassiou, *Vers L'Union Balkanique,* pp. 271-272.
[12] *Les Balkans,* January-February 1934, p. 112.
[13] Papanastassiou, *op. cit.,* p. 276.
[14] *Ibid.,* pp. 276, 280.

the Balkans which has as its goal the forceful or *peaceful* "mutilation" of the present frontiers.[15]

Protest soon arose against the Pact. Bulgarians saw in it a lever to force them to renounce all hope of territorial readjustment.[16] Venizelos and his followers in Greece bitterly assailed it on the ground that it would involve the Balkans in extra-Balkan wars, and would compromise Greece's amicable relations with the Great Powers.[17] Professor Iorga in Rumania attacked it as a general menace to Rumanian and European peace.[18]

Like most international and political agreements, the Entente is not entirely an unalloyed mixture of good. It is both commendable and condemnable. Here for the first time since the late war is to be found a political grouping of Balkan states, and for the first time in their stormy history an alliance not concluded with the preconceived notion of warring upon one of their neighbours or of forcefully divesting others of their possessions. However, the Pact is only one step removed, for it is obviously designed to prevent any change, whether peaceful or forceful, in the territorial arrangement arrived at at the conclusion of the last war. It is probable that the Entente was inspired to some extent, how much no outsider can tell, by the work and ideas set on foot by the Balkan Conferences and the participants therein. For this the Conferences and the delegates deserve their proper share of praise. In noting Minister Maximos' words that while the signatories had not achieved all that the "apostles of the Balkan idea" desired, but that they had nevertheless

---

[15] Papanastassiou, *op. cit.*, pp. 279, 280.
[16] *New York Times*, 12th February, 1934.
[17] *Les Balkans*, January-February 1934, p. 108.
[18] *Ibid.*, p. 103.

achieved all that the exigencies of the hour would allow, one should recall the compromise resolution which the Rumanians had secured the adoption of at the last Balkan Conference, calling upon the governments to suit the Conference pact to circumstances as best they could. If this Pact of Entente represents such an honest effort its authors ought not to be too severely criticised for their handiwork. But, it does seem at least a bit strange that if the drafters had a real intention of making this Pact a first, though imperfect step in the directon of the type of union the Conferences have had in mind, some reference to such a hope or idea might have found expression in the Preamble, which after all has no binding force in international law. Of course, Article 3 says that the Pact is open to all Balkan states, and in this respect differs from the Little Entente treaties. However, this does not alter the force of the observation that there is lacking any mention of the desirability or plan for ultimate union or organization of any sort beyond the mere provision for consultation "in case of eventualities capable of affecting their interests as defined in this agreement" to be to "guarantee the security of all of their Balkan frontiers."

If the Pact of Entente has drawn anything from the draft pact of the Conference, it has drawn upon the articles relating to territorial *status quo,* and mutual assistance.

It is obvious that the Balkan Entente, as enunciated in this Pact, represents an extension of the philosophy and policies of the Little Entente into the Balkans.[19]

---

[19] *Les Balkans,* January-February 1934, p. 100, citing *Le Temps,* semi-official organ of the French government ; *The Central European Observer,* 23rd March, 1934.

Therefore, it may be interesting to compare this agreement with the Little Entente alliances.[20] In the first place, the Preamble of the Balkan Pact bears a strong resemblance to the Preambles of the three Little Entente treaties. Both start off with mention of the resolve to maintain the peace. Both mention contractual agreements. The Little Entente treaties specifically name the Treaty of Trianon and Hungary. The Balkan Pact uses the less definite but none the less obvious words "assure respect for contractual agreements already existing," of which the unnamed Treaty of Neuilly can be the one uppermost in their minds. In the second place, Article 2 of the Balkan Pact has the same purpose as Articles 2 in each of the alliance treaties regarding concert upon measures of action, even though the alliances use the words "competent Technical Authorities." There can be no doubt that military conversations and planning are involved in both cases. In the third place, both sets of agreements are almost identical, word for word, on the limitation placed upon each of the signatories respecting the conclusion of treaties or agreements with other states. In this matter it should be observed that in Article 4 of the Rumanian-Yugoslavian alliance provision is made for consultation on matters of policy affecting Bulgaria, a state not included in either Entente.

The Balkan Pact was not copied from the Little Entente alliances, and it is not as advanced as the Little Entente Pact of Organization of February 1933.[20a] But, as hinted above in connection with the diplomatic visitation which preceded the signing of the Pact, it

[20] See Appendix III.
[20a] See Appendix VI.

does seem as if it were not only inspired by these treaties, but as if it were some kind of attempt to bring the Balkans into alignment with France and the Little Entente, either as a satellite or as an associate. Subsequent developments seem to give further evidence of the one or the other of these views.

While Yugoslavia has been a loyal supporter of these policies in Central Europe, she acceded to this Pact with some hesitancy. Italy, Hungary, Bulgaria, and Albania all harbour grievances or designs against Yugoslavia. It is not without passing interest that no one of these powers is included in the list of signatories. The Little Entente treaties provide enough prophylaxis to take care of Hungary or Bulgaria in case of unilateral hostilities by either one against Yugoslavia. But they do not provide enough should either or both of these powers be aided, as would conceivably be the case, by Italian and Albanian action. From numerous indications it would appear that during 1933 and 1934 King Alexander's foreign policy was designed to remove Bulgaria from the Italian sphere of influence, settle the major differences with her, and get an agreement which would leave Yugoslavia free to deal with her three other neighbours without fear of hostilities in the Balkans. One notes that in the Balkan press, the Belgrade papers expressed regret over Bulgarian absence from the Pact and a desire for early participation.[21] One also notes the lack of any outbreak of public opinion against Yugoslavia in Bulgaria following the announcement of the Pact, and that negotiations between the two countries continued without a hitch. It is rumoured that the provision for denunciation at the end of two years in

[21] *Les Balkans*, January-February 1934, p. 105.

the supplementary agreement was a concession by the other powers to Yugoslavia, which threatened to withdraw from signature of the Pact when Bulgaria made known her decision. Yugoslavian ratification indicated on the one hand that the Bulgarian negotiations had not yet reached the stage of a neutrality agreement, much less an alliance. The lukewarmness and studied vagueness adopted in Belgrade pointed out, on the other hand, a clear-cut aim of avoiding provocation to Sofia, and uncertainty as to the general wisdom and usefulness of such a treaty in the achievement of the larger goals of her foreign policy as well as a certain measure of internal disagreement on foreign policies. It contributed nothing to the settlement of the Yugoslav-Bulgarian problems. It afforded no sure military aid in case of war with Hungary and/or Italy.

Greece and Turkey, while sharing the universal trepidation about war, may, perhaps, have had other motives for favouring such a treaty. The wording of Article 1 is strikingly the same as that of Article 1 of the Græco-Turkish Pact of Entente Cordiale noted earlier. The latter understanding, it will be recalled, was aimed at preventing any territorial modification of the Thracian frontier. One wonders if the Greeks and Turks, seeing the Bulgarian-Yugoslavian questions advancing toward solution, did not fear that Bulgarian and Yugoslavian diplomacy would soon direct their combined forces for the creation of a corridor or corridors out to the Ægean, which Yugoslavia would need in the event of war with Italy. The Greeks might also fear that the two powers would unite to resolve the Macedonian problem by forcing Greece to relinquish part of her Macedonian territory.

Rumania, too, may have had an ulterior interest in the conclusion of such a Pact. If war should be precipitated in Western Europe it would almost inevitably involve Hungary and Rumania in a new struggle for Transylvania. Bulgaria, in spite of constant professions of peace, might conceivably enlist her support on the side of Germany and Hungary as before, to the embarrassment of Rumanian operations.[21a] An alliance would produce Greek and Turkish intervention against Bulgaria in such a case. A second more immediate Rumanian interest would resemble that actuating Greece and Turkey. Amity between Bulgaria and Yugoslavia might result not only at the expense of Greece and Turkey, but of Rumania as well, for Bulgaria has not forgotten the alienation of the southern Dobrudja with its Bulgarian population and outlet to the Black Sea. Reconciliation with Yugoslavia would free Bulgaria to work for the eventual reacquisition of this territory upon which Rumania has lavished much effort since 1921.

In spite of assertions within and without the Balkans that the Pact was not directed against any power,[22] it would be absurd to believe that such an agreement would have been made without some purpose or objective. An analysis of the recent history and policies of the nations of Central and Eastern Europe can leave little doubt in the mind of any neutral observer which of the unnamed parties the framers must have had in mind. That at least one party recognized the direction of the Pact, and that efforts had been made to prevent its signature, was made clear in an interpellation in the

---

[21a] The mission of General Goering to Sofia in June 1935 indicated the aim of German policy in this direction.

[22] Papanastassiou, *op. cit.*, p. 225.

Hungarian Parliament. Asked why he had not prevented the conclusion of the Balkan Pact, Premier Gömbos replied that not even a major power had been able to do so, let alone himself.[23]

There is another characteristic of the Athens instrument : the vagueness and generality of the obligations assumed under Article 2. The parties agree "to concert on the measures to be taken in the presence of eventualities affecting those interests which they have defined in the present accord." What kinds of "measures" are to be taken? Are they to be measures of peaceful action, or may they involve military and hostile activity? What kinds of "eventualities" affect the stipulated interests? — Peaceful agitation and propaganda for revision of boundaries ; appeal to the League of Nations for revision in accordance with the Covenant ; failure to suppress armed bands, as the Macedonian revolutionaries ; or only actual armed violation of the frontiers ? Do the "eventualities" include activities originating outside of the Balkan peninsula, or are they confined to the actions of Balkan states, and if so, which are the Balkan states?

This vagueness and uncertain extent of the contractual obligations gave rise to vehement opposition, especially in Greece. M. Venizelos held that Greek ratification would involve a fundamental change in Greece's historic policy of friendship with all. Greece, he argued, should not ratify such an instrument until it was satisfactory to and accepted by her two neighbours, Albania and Bulgaria. It was also maintained that ratification would embroil Greece in a war between Yugoslavia and Italy, regardless of the merits of the

[23] *Central European Observer*, 18th May, 1934.

case.[24] This opposition was undoubtedly designed to produce a clarification of the treaty. But it seems also to have been due in part at least to news having leaked to the opposition leaders of important secret conversations and an understanding having been reached by Turkey, Rumania, and Soviet Russia just prior to the signature of the Pact. Before the final conference on the Pact at Zagreb, the Soviet Ambassador to Turkey is said to have called the attention of the Turkish government to the fact that if Turkey should sign the Pact and then trouble should develop between Rumania and Russia over Bessarabia, Turkey would be forced to side with Rumania against Russia, in violation of the Russo-Turkish treaty of friendship and neutrality.[25] Convinced of the probity of the Russian argument, the Turkish government seems to have instructed its representative to point out to Rumania its embarrassing position and to demand reconsideration before signature. According to the correspondent of the *New York Times*, "the Rumanian Foreign Minister overcame the difficulty by offering to the Turkish Foreign Minister a written declaration to the effect that should such a contingency as that suggested by the Soviet Union arise Rumania would not expect Turkey to come to her aid."[26]

To answer the opposition in Greece and elsewhere, the signatories conferred and then issued a series of "official interpretations." It was announced by both Maximos and Twefik Rushdi Bey that the Pact had been called to the attention of the major governments — Britain, France, Hungary, Italy, and Russia — and

[24] *New York Times*, 2nd March, 1934 ; *ibid.*, 18th March, 1934. *Les Balkans*, January-February 1934, p. 108 et seq.
[25] *New York Times*, 18th March, 1934.
[26] *Ibid.*

received their approbation.[27] Jevtich said in the Yugoslavian chamber that the Pact was in no way to be interpreted as an alliance directed at any power or powers, directly or indirectly.[28] The most far-reaching declaration and "official interpretation" was made by Maximos in the Greek chamber. Declaring that it was strictly in line with the Geneva policy of regional agreements, he said, "The Balkan Entente Pact has for its end only the guaranteeing of the security of the intra-Balkan frontiers against an aggression coming from any Balkan State. As a result, Greece would not be involved by the commitments assumed in virtue of the Pact, in a war against any Great Power."[29]

Opposition to the Pact was satisfied with the declarations, and ratifications proceeded in the various capitals. However, the declaration of M. Maximos does not entirely answer the charges of M. Venizelos that Greece would become involved in a war with Italy. If Italy should, for instance, back Albania and Bulgaria in a campaign to revise their "intra-Balkan frontiers," Greece and the other states would most assuredly find themselves ranged against Italy. The declaration is not so specific as that between Turkey, Rumania, and Russia, nor can it be in the absence of a written understanding between Greece, Italy, Albania, and Bulgaria. In spite of the declaration, Greece is in greater danger of becoming an enemy to Italy than heretofore, and the more so because Yugoslavia would be required to go

---

[27] *Les Balkans*, March-April 1934, pp. 284, 293 ; *ibid.*, January-February 1934, p. 100 ; Papanastassiou, *op. cit.*, p. 225.

[28] *Les Balkans*, March-April 1934, pp. 293-294.

[29] *Ibid.*, pp. 282-285 ; *New York Times*, 18th March, 1934 ; *The Near East and India*, 29th March, 1934, p. 246. Inferentially, this would hold true for each of the signatory states.

to the aid of Greece against Albania and/or Bulgaria should they get into trouble, and Yugoslavian entry into the picture would almost certainly bring in its train Italian hostilities.

The official declarations fail to do another thing. They do not clarify the commitments assumed, either in Article 1 or Article 2. They do not outline the "eventualities" which might call for action, nor do they announce in any way other than by negative inference the type of "measures" to be taken. By stating that they would not be involved in war with any "Great Power," they nevertheless infer that war might be a measure against a state not a "Great Power." The vagueness of the entire proposition leads to the belief that among the signatories there must be some secret or supplementary agreement. Though constantly denied, the existence of such an agreement became apparent in April 1934, with the publication of the reputed terms in Bulgaria, Britain, and the United States. According to a despatch to the *New York Times* from London "the signatories drew up and signed the protocol in the belief that the Covenant of the League of Nations on which the main pact was based might at some future date not provide the adequate protection it professed and accordingly agreed among themselves to make a subsidiary arrangement which would have a better chance of being operative. The protocol is intended to define the nature of the engagements which these powers have entered and to 'stipulate that these definitions form an integral part of the pact.' " [30]

The terms of the secret protocol, confirmed by M. Mouchanov, and published in the *Zora* at Sofia, 18th

[30] *New York Times*, 26th April, 1934.

March, 1934 are as follows : "Article 1.— Any State will be considered an Aggressor which commits any of the actions defined in Article 2 of the Convention defining the Aggressor, of July 3, 1933. Article II.— The Pact is directed against no Power, but is intended to guarantee the security of Balkan frontiers against acts of aggression by Balkan States. Article III.— Should a Signatory be attacked by a non-Balkan State, and should the latter be supported by a Balkan State, the Pact will come into operation against that Balkan State. Article IV.— The Signatories must conclude within six months Conventions providing for the execution of the terms of the Pact. Article V.— The Pact does not conflict with agreements previously concluded and published by the Signatories. Article VI.— The Signatories will respect all previous agreements signed by them. Article VII.— The Pact is defensive and would not operate in favour of a Signatory committing an act of aggression. Article VIII.— The Pact is intended to preserve the *status quo* in the Balkans. Its duration will be determined within the ensuing two years, and in the meantime no denunciation is permissible. If, at the end of two years, no duration is fixed, the Pact will be renewed automatically for a further five years ; and upon expiry of that term, if still undenounced, it will be automatically renewed for a further equal period." [31]

The terms of the "secret protocol" — there seems to be little reason for keeping them secret — clear up some of the uncertainties of the Pact, but leave others still shrouded in doubt. Articles I and II help to clarify the

[31] *The Near East and India*, 5th April, 1934, p. 267; Digest of terms in the *New York Times*, 26th April, 1934, and the *Eleftheron Vima* (Athens), 21st March, 1934.

objectives of the Pact, but add little to the status of affairs created by the London Conventions. Without questioning the propriety of defining an aggression in these precise terms, their inclusion in the Balkan Pact made Bulgarian adherence difficult so long as the Macedonian Organization remained legal in Bulgaria and persisted in its unlawful terroristic activities. Taking for granted the correctness of such a principle it is interesting that more of a stir was not created in Sofia upon the announcement of this alliance system which ties the other Balkan states into a unit against such activities. The absence of any loud protest gives additional validity to the belief that far-reaching assurances were given to the Bulgarians by some power or powers and that the Bulgarians themselves were reaching the parting of the ways with the I.M.R.O. At any rate, Bulgaria should not find adherence an insuperable obstacle when it is recalled that Austria made an agreement with Czechoslovakia under somewhat similar conditions in the Treaty of Lany, 16th December, 1921.[32] Coupled with this may be the explanation for the unusually brief term of initial duration specified in Article VIII. It is said that the two year clause was inserted upon the request of Yugoslavia, with an eye to a broader Balkan Pact embracing Bulgaria.[33]

Article III pledges the parties to do exactly what M. Venizelos warned they would have to do, and the "official interpretations" denied, namely: go to war against a non-Balkan state. Four types of situations can be imagined : (a) one Balkan state attacks

[32] Machray, *op. cit.*, p. 181.
[33] *Foreign Policy Reports* (New York), 9th May, 1934, p. 64 ; see pages 98-99, *ante.*

another ; (b) a non-signatory Balkan state attacks a
signatory, either with or without foreign support ; (c)
a non-Balkan state attacks a Balkan state with a Balkan
state as an ally ; and (d) a non-Balkan state attacks a
Balkan state, unsupported by any Balkan state or *vice
versa*. In only the last instance would the entente not
be binding, and that is an instance still relatively hard
to imagine. Extra-Balkan attack would probably come
from only three sources, and in the case of aggression
from any one of these sources, the political and military
situation of the Balkans is still such that there is considerable probability that the foreign attack would
sooner or later be supported by Balkan aid of a sort
which would bring it within the scope of those "eventualities" suggested by the Pact.

Article IV leaves Article II of the Pact still in doubt,
and will continue to do so until the exact terms of the
conventions are made known.

In affirming the compatibility of the Pact with previous agreements to which the parties are signatories
Articles V and VI would seem to leave the door open
for appeal to the League of Nations for revision of
frontiers under the terms of the Covenant. While this
is doubtless calculated to appeal to Bulgarian and allied
opinion, it is robbed of considerable value in view of the
attitude which the parties adopted toward the League in
concluding the secret protocol.

In *fine,* what may be said for and against the Balkan
Pact of Entente? In the first place, it is a sequel to the
1933 London agreements defining an aggressor. It
endeavours to apply collective sanctions in place of
vicarious enforcement. In the second place, it represents an extension of the philosophy and system of the

Little Entente into the Balkans.   In the third place, it perhaps marks the beginning of an official movement toward international organization in the Balkans.   Despite the fact that the Pact is a partial one; that it does not embrace all Balkan states ; that it has taken into account none of the Conference suggestions regarding pacific settlement, minorities, or economic, social, and intellectual organization ; that it looks like a return to the old pre-war alliance system, the Entente should not be too severely prejudged.   *"L'art politique c'est l'art du possible."*   If, as seems possible from subsequent events which will be traced presently, this marks the first move toward official adoption of the idea of Balkan unification it deserves hearty support.   However, it may well be agreed that a genuine pact of *union* when it is considered is not to be "lightly drafted by perambulating Foreign Ministers during visits of two or three days' duration to different capitals.   It calls for the intensive work, extending over many months of an official Balkan Conference, at which the plenipotentiaries of the six countries will thresh out, free from all publicity until a draft Pact can be submitted, the details of a system which will unite the Balkan peoples as a single political and economic unit, for all intents and purposes, in the comity of nations." [34]

II

BEFORE following the sequence of official acts farther, it may be well to consider the effect of the Balkan Pact of Entente upon the Conference movement.   The meeting of the Balkan Council, originally scheduled for

[34] *The Near East and India,* 22nd February, 1934, p. 143.

January, was finally held the last of March, having been postponed out of deference to the diplomatic negotiations under way at that time. Immediately upon assembling, the Council was plunged into confusion, largely as a result of the signature of the Balkan Pact of Entente. Albania was not represented, and, to make matters worse, informed the Council of her complete withdrawal from the organization. The Bulgarians threatened to follow suit, and the Yugoslavians showed considerable restiveness.

M. Papanastassiou as President of the Council, called upon the Albanians to reconsider their action. The Conference, he again argued, was a semi-private organization and as such unable to control the acts of the states. Furthermore, he pointed out, all national groups had protested against the slight to Albania.[35] A resolution was unanimously adopted by the Council urging the Albanian group to continue its membership and collaboration,[36] but without result. The Albanians sulked, and during 1934 the relations between Albania and Greece became materially embittered.[37]

Prolonged discussion then arose from a suggestion of M. Yovanovitch of the Yugoslavian group, that there was now less work for the Conference to do and that the next Conference be adjourned *sine die* until all six groups could get together, and that at any rate, the next Conference could not be invited to meet in Yugoslavia.[38] The proposal for adjournment was combated on the grounds that the statute required annual meet-

[35] *Les Balkans*, March-April 1934, p. 298.
[36] *Ibid*, p. 299.
[37] *New York Times*, 18th November, 1934.
[38] *Les Balkans, supra*, p. 300.

ings, that the mere guaranteeing of frontiers did not assure peace, and that instead of less work to be done there was far more now necessary.[39]

While this discussion was progressing, the Bulgarians proceeded to throw a bombshell into the meeting by advancing two questions for which, as the price of their vote for *sine die* adjournment or continuance of the Conferences, they demanded an immediate and categorical answer from each delegation. The questions which they posed for all the delegations were:

"I. — Do they approve, yes or no, the Four Power Pact which has been signed, a partial Pact and directed at other countries of the Peninsula ?

"II. — Are they disposed to bring to light the secret clauses of the Pact, the contradictions between its stipulations and the aspirations of the Conference, and, in the affirmative case, would they be willing to take on themselves the task of recommending to their respective Governments the conclusion of pacts of non-aggression which would permit the Conference to persevere in its efforts to realize a political and economic unity of the Balkan States ?" [40]

These questions aroused much discussion and feeling, though a direct answer was evaded by all. M. Yovanovich followed the line of reasoning he had already advanced, arguing that this move was further substantiation of his proposal that the Conference be adjourned. M. Papanastassiou tried to appease the Bulgarians without answering them, saying that he regarded the Yugoslavian argument as clearly for termination of the efforts of the Conference whereas the Bulgarian move was one for intensification of the work of the movement.

[39] *Les Balkans*, March-April 1934, pp. 301-303.
[40] *Ibid.*, p. 304.

M. Pella of Rumania sought to reconcile both the Yugoslavs and the Bulgarians, also without answering the questions, asserting that the adoption of the Yugoslavian proposal would only add to the isolation and misunderstanding which the Pact had already created, and he, therefore, suggested that instead of meeting at Belgrade the fifth Conference meet at Istanbul, to which the Turks gave their hearty endorsement. But neither of these arguments sufficed to satisfy either the Bulgarians or the Yugoslavians, and on the final vote whether to hold the fifth Conference or to adjourn *sine die,* the Bulgarians and Yugoslavians voted to adjourn, and the Greeks, Rumanians, and Turks voted to continue.[41] This did not augur well for the fifth Conference or for the future of the movement which, in the brief span of four years had gone deeper into the fundamental ills of the Balkans and gone farther in suggesting means of progress than all the diplomatic and international acts of seven centuries.

The Council continued with its pre-determined schedule in spite of the shock which it had sustained, and credit must be given to both the Bulgarian and Yugoslavian delegates for their remaining at the Council and aiding its subsequent work. This loyal and democratic act helped to dispel some fears and evidenced an appreciation of the fundamental aims of the Conferences. In 1933 several had favoured converting the Balkan Conference into an official or semi-official organ. This idea was recurred to in the Council, and, as a means of preventing a complete breakdown of the movement and of enlisting additional governmental support as well as making the necessary transition easier, it was

[41] *Les Balkans,* March-April 1934, pp. 304-307.

proposed for consideration by the Conference that the organization be changed to the *Union Parlementaire et Sociale Balkanique* and that the seat of the union be permanently fixed at Istanbul.[42]   All groups joined in assenting to this suggestion, thus further healing the break in the ranks.   This action was followed by the establishment of committees to codify the Conference resolutions, inaugurate educational weeks, and to co-ordinate the activities of co-operative societies.   Balkan Weeks were provided for with the customary conferences in the various capitals.[43]

The agenda which was drawn up for the fifth Conference with the assent of all delegations provided for a continuation of the broad analysis and study of the Balkan problems much as at the previous Conferences.[44] It was proposed that the Political Commission consider the reconciliation of the Pact of Entente, the Draft Pact, a Pact of Non-Aggression and ultimate federation.

Disrupted, the Council adjourned having fulfilled its statutory tasks but rather the worse for its experience.

The Yugoslavian proposal for adjournment was again pressed in the summer of 1934 but not acceded to until after the assassination of King Alexander in October.[45] While this decision was generally regretted by the Conference leaders, it was not felt that it implied a complete termination of their work.

III

THE signature of the Pact did not put a stop to the attempts of Yugoslavia to reach an understanding with

[42] *Les Balkans*, March-April 1934, p. 307.
[43] *Ibid*, p. 308.
[44] *Ibid.*, pp. 308-310.
[45] *New York Times*, 14th October, 1934, p. E3.

Bulgaria. Nor did the Entente remain hollow and meaningless, restricted only to questions concerning frontiers.

Shortly after a visit of the Foreign Minister of Yugoslavia to Sofia in May a highly significant *coup d'état* took place in Bulgaria as a result of which a military dictatorship was set up, favourably inclined toward Yugoslavia, the Little Entente and France.[46] This government was "warmly welcomed" in Belgrade, and favour was shown by the immediate conclusion of a commercial treaty.[47] The Macedonians were not only forced out of the government but forcibly dissolved or run out of the country, to the apparent relief of both Bulgarians and Yugoslavians.[48] The reconciliation between the two states was carried a step further through the visit of King Alexander and Queen Marie to Sofia in September.[49] Little has been revealed of what transpired between the governments during this visit, although agreement has been reported upon the opening of the frontier and upon passport regulations.[50] It cannot be said that an entente or alliance was reached by the two states, — Yugoslavia would have to have had the consent of the members of the Balkan Entente for that, and there is no evidence that such was given. However, the foundations for an entente may have been laid. It cannot be affirmed that Bulgaria was asked, much less persuaded, to enter the Balkan Entente though it is inconceivable that discussion of that topic was not included in the conversations. Bulgarian adherence

---

[46] *New York Times*, 20th May, 1934.
[47] *The Near East and India*, 31st May, 1934, p. 419.
[48] *New York Times*, 26th August, 1934.
[49] *Ibid.*, 28th September, 1934.
[50] *Foreign Policy Bulletin*, New York, 5th October, 1934.

involves territorial adjustments and concessions which Serbian, Greek, and Rumanian officialdom, especially military, may not yet be ready to make. King Alexander is known to have favoured the cession of part of Serbian Macedonia,[51] and Foreign Minister Titulescu is reported to have assured Bulgaria of his readiness to help her secure an outlet to the Ægean,[52] so that forces are on foot to reconcile Bulgaria and make the entente all-Balkan. However, there are sinister forces driving in the other direction which are by no means ready to accept such a program.[53]

If the Balkan Entente slumbered during the summer months of 1934, it jumped to life after the assassination of King Alexander, perhaps to the consternation of the unseen instigators of the October murder. A meeting of the ministers of the Balkan Entente was held, along with a meeting of the ministers of the Little Entente, at the time of Alexander's funeral. Significantly, a joint *communiqué* was issued by the two Ententes, which bemoaned the assassination, charged that it originated in alien lands, affirmed the solidarity of both groups to Yugoslavia, and pledged them to pursue a unified policy.[54] The similarity between the Little Entente and the Balkan Entente has already been remarked upon. The issuance of this joint announcement was generally accepted as an indication of the complete triumph of the Little Entente over the Balkans and their absorption into its political hegemony. While there can be little doubt of the general identity of their views and policies

---

[51] See statement by Wm. R. Castle, former Under Secretary of State, *New York Times*, 11th October, 1934.

[52] *The Near East and India*, 29th November, 1934, p. 937.

[53] *Christian Century*, New York, 9th January, 1935, p. 41.

[54] *Les Balkans*, October-November 1934, p. 625.

on the preservation of the Neuilly and Trianon treaty settlements, it would appear to be an unwarranted conclusion that the Balkan group has become or intends to become a mere vassal of the Little Entente. At their meeting in Ankara in November, the Balkan ministers emphatically denied any absorption into the Little Entente and firmly asserted the Balkan Entente's control of its own action in all matters.

The Entente did not rest with the mere issuance of a communication after Alexander's death. It proceeded to hold an important meeting at Ankara in Turkey, October 30th-November 2nd. This was considered to be the second "regular" meeting of the Entente, the first having been held at Athens when the Pact was signed. The first meeting, it will be recalled, had been devoted largely to speeches and festivities, so that the Ankara gathering was the first one at which the ministers had an opportunity to get down to work and to demonstrate the real sincerity of their intentions. At this meeting the ministers moved forward in the direction pointed by the Balkan Conferences. They agreed upon immediate action to bring Albania and Bulgaria within the framework of the Balkan Entente, which appears to have evoked a favourable response in Sofia.[55] A permanent secretariat, resembling that of the Little Entente and of the Balkan Conference, was set up. An Economic Commission was instituted, with orders to meet twice before the next assemblage of the Council at Bucharest in May, 1934, for the consideration of establishing closer trade relations, the development of communications, especially on the Danube and Black Sea, the founding of a Balkan bank, and the stimulation

[55] See dispatch from Sofia in *New York Times*, 30th October, 1934.

of the tourist trade. A second commission, suggested
by the murder of Alexander, was charged with exchang-
ing information and promoting collaboration among the
Balkan police services. Another commission was established to consider the unification of Balkan laws.[56]

All of these decisions and actions are directly in line
with the recommendations of the Balkan Conferences.
Upon each of the subjects for study by the Entente's
commissions, the Balkan Conferences have already
assembled an elaborate documentation and themselves
conducted debates, so that the work of the Entente
should be greatly facilitated. In addition to these matters, the Entente considered at length, and finally voted
adherence to the Argentine Anti-War Pact.[57] Here
again, the Council was acceding in principle at least to
the requests of the Balkan Conferences for the conclusion of a non-aggression and pacific settlement
convention.

The terms of this Anti-War Treaty on Non-Aggression and Conciliation, originally intended to be purely
a Pan-American affair but now ratified by thirty states,
may be found in the Appendix. The Preamble to the
treaty does not differ materially, in purpose at least,
from the ideas expressed in the Preamble to the Conference's Draft Pact, or the General Act of Pacific
Settlement of the Little Entente. It condemns wars
of aggression and territorial acquisitions obtained by
armed conquest. Considering the philosophy and purposes expressed in the Pact of Entente, it is easy to
understand why the Balkan ministers would favour this

[56] *Les Balkans*, October-November 1934, pp. 626-630 ; *Geneva, Monthly
Review of International Affairs*, November 1934, p. 112 ; *The Near East
and India*, 22nd November, 1934, p. 918.
[57] *New York Times*, 20th December, 1934.

treaty. In Article One of the treaty the parties contract to "condemn" wars of aggression among themselves or with other states, and "declare" that the settlement of "disputes or controversies of any kind that may arise among them shall be effected only by pacific means which have the sanction of international law." It is to be noted that the agreement with respect to war is narrower and less binding here than in the Kellogg-Briand Pact where war is "renounced." Neither Article One nor subsequent articles forbid warfare or render it illegal. It should also be observed that while wars are condemned mutually and toward other parties, the measures of pacific settlement are to apply only as between the high contracting parties. If the latter part of the article — "pacific means which have the sanction of international law" — is to be taken at its face value, settlement may be achieved not only by arbitration, conciliation, conferences, diplomacy, good offices, judicial settlement or mediation, but also by the employment of boycotts, embargo, display of force, intervention, non-intercourse, pacific blockade, reprisals and retorsion. In fact, disputes may be settled by apparently any method short of "wars of aggression." The Argentine Pact marks progress, even for the Balkans, but it still leaves room for a continuance of that anarchic system aptly designated as "Force in Peace." [58]

Article Two contains a declaration, not an agreement. The parties declare territorial questions must not be settled by "violence." The article then adopts the Hoover-Stimson doctrine applied to Manchuria, to the effect that the parties will not "recognize" any terri-

[58] Hindmarsh, A., *Force in Peace*, Cambridge, 1933.

torial arrangement not obtained by pacific means, nor
the occupation of land "brought about by force of arms."
It is easy to understand the readiness of the Balkan
Entente to adopt this declaration.   It is directly in line
with the terms of their own pact.   However, it is worth
calling attention to the fact that the limitation on
readjustments applies not to states in general, but "as
between the high contracting parties."   There is much
to quibble over in this article, but one thing is sure : as
between the present members of the Entente there is
little or no controversy over territorial arrangements.
Turkey and Greece are the only ones that are likely to
have serious altercations over boundaries, and they have
already mutually guaranteed the security of their
frontier by their treaty of 1933.   However, if Bulgaria
and Albania join the Entente the situation would be
different.   But, significantly enough, Bulgaria too, has
deposited her ratification of this treaty independently of
the Entente.[59]   The treaty does not make clear whether
"violence," "not obtained by pacific means," and "force
of arms" refer to hostile and belligerent action, or action
in time of peace.   Ordinarily the use of "violence" and
"force of arms" for the *de facto* and *de jure* acquisition
of land are legal only in time of war.   Where pacific
blockades, intervention, reprisals, and display of force
are employed, they are used when full diplomatic relations continue.   And it is not the intervention of troops,
or the display of force which changes boundaries or
acquires territory, but the diplomatic arm of the government through negotiation.   And all of these methods
are entirely justifiable pacific means with the sanction
of international law under Article One.

[59] *New York Times*, 20th December, 1934.

The Draft Pact of the Conference was slightly clearer and more binding than the Argentine Treaty in this matter. According to its Article One, there was a definite contract among the parties. It provided that none of the parties should "attack," "invade," or "have recourse to war" to settle issues. It seems reasonably clear that "violence," non-pacific means, and use of "force of arms" would embrace attack, invasion, and war.

In the conference Draft Pact the parties agreed to take "all necessary measures" to fulfill the obligations of non-aggression. The mutual assistance articles provided for calling the matter to the attention of the League Council for immediate action, and/or, as the violation might be a flagrant one, going at once "to the aid of" the party against which a violation or contravention had unprovokedly been directed, when that party had satisfactorily demonstrated that the action was unprovoked and involved "crossing of the frontiers," or "the opening of hostilities." Article Three of the Argentine Pact substitutes an entirely different concept and system, one quite new to the post-war world. The article sets forth that in case of non-compliance with the preceding articles "by any State engaged in a dispute," the "contracting States" undertake "to make every effort for the maintenance of peace." The article then continues to its significant part. It provides, in its own words, "To that end they will adopt in their character as neutrals a common and solidary attitude ; they will exercise the political, juridical or economic means authorized by international law ; they will bring the influence of public opinion to bear but will in no case resort to intervention either diplomatic or armed ;

subject to the attitude that may be incumbent on them by virtue of other collective treaties to which such States are signatories."

This article, in the first place, helps to clear up some of the questions raised by the preceding article. It leaves relatively little doubt but that the "violence" and "force of arms" are only those used in war, for in international law, which the treaty constantly invokes, there can be no neutrality apart from the existence of a state of war. Apparently, therefore, the Balkan states may use any means short of war for the adjustment of territorial issues without provoking the exercise of the sanctions mentioned.

But more significant than this is the form of sanctions provided for by this article. The Covenant of the League of Nations, the Geneva Protocol, the Kellogg-Briand Pact, and all known existing or proposed regional security agreements, make no allowance for, or at least no mention of neutrality in the next war. Under Articles 10 and 16 of the Covenant of the League, the member states have covenanted together to take such measures against an aggressor as the Council may direct, and mutually to "support one another in resisting any special measures aimed at one of their members by the Covenant-breaking State." In a state of war any belligerent, operating under the customary laws of war, against whom such League action was directed would normally regard any such steps by the third states as unneutral and unfriendly.[60] The unratified Treaty of Mutual Assistance of 1919, the

[60] Quincy Wright, "The Future of Neutrality," *International Conciliation*, No. 242 (September 1928) ; E. Stowell, *International Law*, New York, 1931, Bk. III, Pt. I, Chap. 3. See statement of Italian attitude toward League sanctions in *New York Times*, 24th August, 1935.

Little Entente treaties, the Locarno Pact, the Franco-Polish and Franco-Czechoslovak alliances, and proposed Eastern and Mediterranean "Locarnos" all make provision for enlarging the theatre of a war by making neutrality impossible on the part of any of the signatories. Exceptions to this trend have been a series of friendship and neutrality treaties which Soviet Russia, Italy, and Turkey have signed with each other and a few other countries.[61]

This Argentine treaty marks a distinct reversal of the post-war trend. It does not break entirely with the League Covenant system in as much as it provides for the employment of collective political, economic, judicial, and moral pressure upon the recalcitrant power, and leaves room, in its last clause for the commitments of its signatories under the Covenant. However, in stipulating that "in their character as neutrals" they shall "in no case resort to intervention either diplomatic or armed" a very different concept is given application. While the Pact does not embody quite the same principles as the Armed Neutralities of the late eighteenth century, it does adopt the idea of a collective neutrality.[62] If this article could actually be carried out throughout the duration of a war between Great Powers, it would be helpful in narrowing the arena of the conflict rather than universalizing it as in the late war and as sought by the various post-war mutual assistance compacts. Such a restriction of conflicts and elimination of foreign entanglements is directly in line with the general objectives which the Balkan Conferences

[61] See for example, Turkish-Italian treaty of 30th October, 1928, League of Nations, *Treaty Series*, Vol. XCV, p. 183 ; also Greek-Turkish treaty of the 30th October.

[62] *American Journal of International Law*, July, 1934, pp. 540-541.

have been anticipating. However, it seems somewhat doubtful whether the exercise of the various means of pressure upon the violator is entirely compatible with non-diplomatic or armed intervention. Would, for instance, a belligerent consider a common economic boycott and rupture of diplomatic relations neutral action ? Of course if it did not and attacked any one of the parties that party would have complete right to go to war in self-defence without violating this or any other international agreement.

The remaining articles in the Argentine Treaty deal with the submission of disputes to conciliation, the establishment of conciliation commissions, and the procedure of conciliation. These provisions are substantially the same as those relating to conciliation in the Balkan Draft Pact and the Little Entente's General Act. Both the latter instruments, however, go considerably farther toward establishing a complete system of pacific settlement, for, in addition to conciliation, they provide for arbitration, consideration by the League Council, and the World Court, in case the settlement by conciliation is not acceptable. In view of the possibility of disagreement among Balkan statesmen and conciliators, it would seem advisable for the Entente to make provision, by some general act, for the utilization of these other modes of settlement.

The work of the Entente Council was terminated by taking note of the Balkan Conferences, and by the paying of a "notable tribute" to their work in fostering good-will and organization.[63]

The sincerity and efforts of the ministers at the Ankara Council deserve praise. Much was accomplished,

[63] *Les Balkans*, October-November 1934, p. 628.

more than could have been anticipated. A satisfactory basis for collaboration was discovered, and important investigations were put on foot. If followed up in subsequent councils with a corresponding degree of sincerity and desire for organization, it may well be recorded that the Ankara meeting witnessed the transition of the movement from a semi-public to a full-fledged public endeavour. At any rate, the Council meeting stands as one of the major developments in the movement, and its importance may be attributed in no small measure to the effective ground-work of the Conferences.

IV

THE official movement for Balkan organization increased in tempo and scope during 1935, whereas the original Conference system experienced a continued eclipse. It can hardly be said that the work of the semi-official Balkan Conferences and their agencies is completed, although some of their suggestions have been accepted by the states. That the Conferences laid a solid foundation and created fundamentally sound public views toward unity is testified by the fact that the movement has progressed in spite of their suspension, and in spite of political upheavals. Regardless of the disputes arising from time to time between the states, a basically different attitude from that displayed before 1930 prevails in the Balkans. Unfortunately, the public movement is largely, though naturally, concerned with political and economic questions. The important social, intellectual, and personal relations between the peoples remain untouched by the Entente. The continued formation of right attitudes and folkways waits upon the resumption of the semi-public movement. This cannot be neglected for long without causing damage to the general scheme.

The work of the Entente during 1935 may be divided into two phases : (1) the handling of international emergencies ; and (2) the study and progression toward unity. Three international emergencies confronted the Entente and called for united action : (1) the Yugo-slavian-Hungarian dispute over the sheltering of criminal terrorists ; (2) the Greek revolt ; (3) the re-armament of Austria, Hungary, and Bulgaria. The first and last of these crises called for and produced co-ordinated policies by the Little Entente and the Balkan Entente. The Balkan Entente stood with the Little Entente at Geneva and demanded some form of satisfaction and guarantee for Yugoslavia in connection with the sheltering of terrorists at Janka Puszta in Hungary. While it was rumoured that sanctions would be taken against Hungary if satisfaction was not secured at the League of Nations,[64] the Ententes, rather than embarrassing or weakening the League, accepted the mild resolution passed by the Council[65] and did not force a debate upon the subsequent Hungarian reply. The Balkan Entente was naturally interested in the problem of international control of terrorists not only because two of its members border on Hungary, but also because of the patent existence of the problem in the Balkans, and because of the London Convention Defining the Aggressor. In acting as it did in this case the Entente demonstrated the validity of the objection

[64] *The Near East and India*, 27th December, 1934, p. 1048.
[65] *New York Times*, 11th December, 1934.

raised by the Venizelists that the members would be called upon to meddle in extra-Balkan troubles. It foreshadowed, perhaps, along with subsequent events, the ultimate merger of the two Ententes. It also established a useful precedent of vigorous appeal to and support of the League of Nations.

The insurrection in Greece in March 1935, while a decidedly amateurish affair, had its international implications. And the action in this connection was not unrelated to the problem of Bulgarian rearmament which formed a part of the third emergency dealt with. Prior to the outbreak of the insurrection, Greece and Turkey had been slowly increasing their fortifications in the Thracian and Macedonian region [66] in accordance with an agreement between their general staffs,[67] and in anticipation of a possible Bulgarian and even Yugoslavian attempt to gain territorial corridors to the Ægean. Charges and counter-charges in the Bulgarian and Turkish press aggravated suspicions in both states.[68] When the revolt broke out in Greece, Bulgaria immediately strengthened her frontier garrisons. She denied any intention of exploiting her neighbour's troubles, although it was loudly claimed in both Greece and Turkey that Bulgaria would take advantage of the situation and that it was only the existence of the Entente which prevented her from so doing.[69] In spite of the charges, Bulgaria assumed a meticulously correct policy throughout the course of the revolt, and used the armed forces only to guard against any mass incursion

[66] *New York Times*, 26th February, 1935.
[67] *The Near East and India*, 21st March, 1935, p. 341.
[68] *Ibid.*, 10th January, 1935, pp. 35-36.
[69] *L'Europe Nouvelle*, 16th March, 1935, p. 259.

of refugees or the use of its territory as a base for operations.[70]   However, March 7th the Bulgarian representative at the League of Nations electrified the world with the presentation of a "sensational" memorandum regarding Turkish military preparations in Thrace, charging aggressive designs, and requesting immediate action.[71]   Far from producing the form of action anticipated, this brought the Balkan Entente swarming into action.   Pressure descended upon Sofia from every Balkan capital at once, from Geneva, and from the western capitals which were too preoccupied with the German situation to be bothered with trouble in the Balkans, with the result that two days later the memorandum was withdrawn from Geneva,[72] and the minister subsequently relieved of his post.[73]   While this situation demonstrated the celerity and forcefulness with which the Entente might move, and the pressure which it might bring to bear from external sources, it did not show quite the same degree of readiness to subject charges against Entente members to League consideration as it had with regard to charges against non-members.   Although Bulgaria underwent considerable embarrassment, she at least had the pleasure of seeing the Entente squirm when subjected to the same treatment which it had meted out to Hungary in the previous autumn.   Under a permanent structure of peace, the Entente must be ready to allow international investigation of its own acts as readily as those of others.

The third extraordinary matter calling upon the

[70] *The Near East and India,* 21st March, 1935, p. 341.
[71] *New York Times,* 8th March, 1935.
[72] *Ibid.,* 10th March, 1935.
[73] *The Near East and India,* 4th April, 1935, p. 402.

Entente for consideration was the problem of Austrian, Hungarian, but most specifically, Bulgarian rearmament. For several years prior to 1935, general suspicion prevailed in Central and Eastern Europe that the three defeated powers were arming clandestinely. Because the situation had either reached a critical point, or for political reasons, the Entente announced in February at the time of the League Council meeting that it was "considering" a protest regarding illegal Bulgarian rearmament.[74] No protest was made. The situation became radically altered when Austria, Hungary, and Bulgaria followed Germany in asserting their right to rearm,[75] and when the Great Powers at Stresa recommended to "the other States concerned to examine this question with a view to its settlement by mutual agreement. . ."[76] The two Ententes, again acting arm in arm, were in a strategic position. M. Twefik Rushdi Aras, Foreign Minister of Turkey, was President of the League of Nations Council. M. Benes, representing Czechoslovakia and the Little Entente, held a seat on the Council. And M. Titulescu, Rumanian Foreign Minister, was in Geneva on a special protective and investigative mission for the two Ententes. Pressure was put upon the French, who were charged with indifference to the interests of the Eastern allies.[77] Upon arrival at Geneva, M. Laval, French Foreign Minister, denied the charges and declared that he had no idea of taking the affair out of the hands of the Ententes. During the course of the Council session, which had been called to consider the French

[74] *New York Times*, 15th February, 1935.
[75] *The Near East and India*, 11th April, 1935, p. 436.
[76] No. 6 of the Declarations in the Memorandum of April 14th.
[77] *Geneva*, May 1935, p. 47.

memorandum concerning German unilateral violation of the Treaty of Versailles, intense diplomatic manœuvering took place. The Balkan and Little Entente representatives readily associated themselves with the French, recognizing the applicability of the French contention with regard to German action to the situations more immediately concerning them. The fifth point in the French memorandum was couched in useful language : ". . . In a Europe in which the method of unilaterally denouncing international engagements became general, there would soon be no room for any policy but one of force. No negotiation is possible if, while the conversations are proceeding, one of the parties can arbitrarily possess himself of that which is the subject of those conversations ; nor can any negotiation be of service if its results, whatever they may be, can be destroyed at the will of one of the contracting parties." [78] The Ententes were successful in securing a broadening of the Council resolution in such a way that it would be applicable to Austria, Bulgaria, or Hungary should any of those countries take action similar to Germany's. The pertinent part of the resolution, adopted unanimously with the abstention of Denmark, states that : "The Council . . . III — Considering that the unilateral repudiation of international obligations may endanger the very existence of the League of Nations as an organization for maintaining peace and promoting security decides that such repudiation, without prejudice to the application of the measures already provided in international agreements, should, in the event of its having relations to undertakings concerning the security of peoples and the

[78] *Geneva*, May 1935, p. 49.

maintenance of peace in Europe, call into play all appropriate measures on the part of members of the League, and within the framework of the Covenant ; requests the committee composed of . . . to propose for this purpose measures to render the Covenant more effective in the organization of collective security, and to define in particular the economic and financial measures which might be applied should, in the future, a State, whether member of the League of Nations or not, endanger peace by the unilateral repudiation of its international obligations." [79]

While the resolution, in another part, condemned Germany, it did not propose the adoption of any sanctions against her for her action. In reality, therefore, it represented far more of a victory for the Ententes than it did for France, for it anticipated future rather than past actions, and as yet the three non-Entente states have taken no unilateral steps other than to assert the *right* to rearm. Vigorous, forthright moves may be anticipated against any one of these three powers if they openly rearm on any sensational scale for the hand of the Ententes has been measurably strengthened by this move.

But the Balkan Entente went farther. Prior to the vote on the resolution at the closing session on the 18th April, 1935, the Turkish representative announced, without doubt with the full knowledge of his colleagues,[80] that if Austria, Bulgaria, and Hungary were to be allowed to rearm then Turkey would demand and proceed to fortify the Straits.[81] This clever diplomatic

[79] *Geneva*, May 1935, pp. 50-51.
[80] *The Near East and India*, 18th April, 1935, p. 466.
[81] *New York Times*, 18th April, 1935.

move began to produce at once its desired effect, as the British, French and Italian representatives opposed it and entered reservations.[82]   This matter was considered at length by the Balkan Entente Council at its meeting in Bucharest in May.   Difficulties arose from Yugoslavian opposition to any rearmament, and from a general desire to find some method of fortification which would not of itself be contrary to the provisions of the Straits and Lausanne conventions and lay Turkey open to the charge of violation of her agreements.[83]   Yugoslavia eventually agreed to the *quid pro quo* and fortification idea in principle, and Turkey was instructed to prepare a plan to be considered at a special Council meeting in Bucharest the middle of June.   According to a dispatch to the *New York Times,* the following plan was considered by the Entente Council :

"First, concession of the right to a number of transportable coastal batteries.

"Second, the right of defense through transportable artillery and other military units on roads leading to the Straits . . .

"Third, the right to construct underground torpedo tubes on the coast.

"Fourth, the right to have two submarine bases and a certain number of submarines.

"Fifth, the right to have two bases for airplanes and seaplanes.

"Turkey as a Balkan Entente nominee will inform the League of Nations before hand as soon as her preparations for constructing these defenses are in a sufficiently advanced stage to become practicable." [84]

[82] *Geneva,* May 1935, p. 51.
[83] *New York Times,* 14th June, 1935; *The Near East and India,* 16th May, 1935, p. 604.
[84] *New York Times,* 14th June, 1935.

Recalling the British and French concern for the demilitarization of the Straits at the close of the World War, it may be assumed that they will not heedlessly consent to unlimited rearmament by Austria, Bulgaria, and Hungary if the price not only involves further jeopardization of European security but also the fortification of the Straits. The Entente powers have gained considerable security by their association. None of them possesses aggressive territorial motives justifying further increases in armaments either in their own territories or in the non-Entente states. No useful end will be gained by additions. Security will not be advanced if all increase, as all will if one does. Genuine and permanent security will best be obtained by federation and union of all of the states in the region, with progressive demilitarization within the confines of the region under an increasingly virile central government.

The Entente was not entirely preoccupied with international emergencies. Thought was given to the problems of federation within the peninsula, of economic relations, and of relations with other countries. The fourth regular Council meeting was held at Bucharest the middle of May, and was attended by the foreign ministers of the four states. The diplomatic representative of Czechoslovakia in Bucharest attended several sessions, again evidencing the close relation between the two Ententes. Like the meetings of the Little Entente, the ministers first examined the general international situation, and reported in their *communiqué* that there were no grounds for fears regarding peace or the development of good neighbourly relations in the Balkans.[85] The advantage of collaboration with the Little Entente

[85] *Central European Observer*, 31st May, 1935, p. 164.

was stressed, as well as the hope that the "Eastern Locarno" Pact being negotiated by France would be realized.   After considering the Danubian problem and the issues likely to arise at the Rome Conference to deal with that, readiness was expressed to work for the fabrication of a Danubian agreement if the legitimate interests of the several states were respected.[86]

The problem of the inclusion of Bulgaria received extensive consideration, and the Council expressed the sincere hope that the Entente might be extended in the immediate future to all the Balkan states.   According to a dispatch in the *Central European Observer,* the press in Bulgaria reacted favourably to this announcement, although it stated that adherence must be accompanied by rearmament and the giving of fresh guarantees of security.[87]   To mid-summer 1935, the changes in Bulgarian government worked no real alteration in the conciliatory and favourable policy of Bulgaria. Much depends, as was repeatedly pointed out in the Balkan Conferences, upon the policies of Bulgaria's neighbours on the one hand, and upon Bulgaria's internal control of the more extremist elements in the Macedonian group.

The work of the Council in the realm of economic affairs was facilitated by the study and report of the Economics Commission set up at the Ankara meeting in November.   It was emphasized that the time was ripe for the extension of commercial and tourist relations within and without the area.   Approval was given to measures for facilitating exports and imports among the states and the knowledge of Balkan products.   Sug-

---

[86] *Central European Observer,* 31st May, 1935.
[87] *Ibid.,* p. 165.

gestions were also adopted for regulating financial and foreign exchange transactions, although the Council did not found, as had been anticipated, a Balkan Bank. With respect to this, it submitted a proposition to the national banks and called a joint conference with the governors of the banks. In substance, the proposed bank will resemble the Bank for International Settlements at Basle. The states were urged to adhere to the postal union, inaugurated under the auspices of the Conferences. The relinquishment of certain passport and police difficulties for the stimulation of tourist travel was also recommended, together with the suggestion that an aviation convention be concluded to aid civil air transportation by the elimination of forbidden zones, and the construction of airways and landing fields. The states were also requested to improve the other modes of transportation.[88]

In all of these political, economic and communications propositions, the Council was following closely upon the paths blazed by the Balkan Conferences, thereby attesting to the validity of their work and recommendations. It would be fortunate indeed, if the Council would request the Conferences to resume their studies and associate their efforts with its own. Much can be gained through the further stimulation of this unofficial movement.

During the year the Balkan states made considerable progress outside the Council in co-operative endeavours, Turkey and Greece created an organization for the promotion and regulation of exports, particularly of tobacco, raisins, and wines.[89] Greece and Bulgaria

---

[88] *Central European Observer*, 31st May, 1935, p. 164.
[89] *The Near East and India*, 3rd January, 1935, p. 8.

settled a long-standing dispute regarding Bulgarian liability for expropriated state property in the Rhodope Mountains.[90] Bulgaria and Rumania established a commission to work on the problem of a bridge or car ferry across the Danube at Giurgiu-Russe.[91] Rumania and Yugoslavia negotiated regarding a bridge across the river also, but reached an impasse when the Yugoslavians insisted upon a tunnel instead of a bridge.[92] Turkey and Yugoslavia set up an organization to control and handle the export of opium, excepting non-medicinal opium destined to the Far East.[93] Bulgaria and Yugoslavia put into effect simplifications of frontier formalities, and opened several more crossing places, in accordance with the agreement reached by Alexander and Boris in 1934.[94] During the Greek revolt, the Turkish authorities cooperated with Greek authorities in detaining ships and cargoes destined to rebel ports.[95] Both Bulgaria and Yugoslavia improved highways leading to the Greek frontier. While these are largely for strategic purposes, they also serve commercial ends and are in accord with the suggestions made for the improvement of communications.[96] Bulgaria and Turkey concluded a commercial treaty and renewed their non-aggression compact.[97]

[90] *The Near East and India*, 10th January, 1935, p. 30.
[91] *Ibid.*, p. 31.
[92] *Ibid.*, 24th January, 1935, p. 88.
[93] *Ibid.*, 17th January, 1935, p. 117.
[94] *Ibid.*, 21st March, 1935, p. 342.
[95] *Ibid.*, 28th March, 1935, p. 373.
[96] *Ibid.*, 21st March, 1935, p. 341 ; *ibid.*, 18th April, 1935, p. 491.
[97] *Ibid.*, 6th June, 1935, p. 693.

v

THE problems which lie immediately ahead of the Entente will not prove easy of solution. The first and most essential step to be taken must be that of winning the co-operation and inclusion of Albania and Bulgaria. This will be difficult for both countries are subject to foreign influences different from those of the other Balkan states. Italian diplomacy and imperialism must be reckoned with in dealing with Albania. German influence must be handled in connection with Bulgaria. It cannot be said that the Entente is a tool of France. There is no denial, however, of the fact that as a combination it is more inclined to France and French diplomatic schemes than it is to either Germany or Italy. The latter countries are definitely interested in expanding their power and control in the Balkans, and the winning of Albania and Bulgaria to union independent of and even opposed to the policies of those states will be a major diplomatic feat but one quite worth the effort entailed.

The second task facing the Entente is related to the first. It must make itself independent of foreign influence, at least of divisive foreign influence. It must make Balkan unity a more desirable and profitable end than foreign favouritism. This work involves, as the Conferences pointed out, freeing the several countries from financial, economic, and cultural dependency as well as from political connections. The Entente must terminate the era of foreign exploitation and imperialism. It must stimulate and free intra-peninsula commerce and life and impose common restraints on extra-Balkan inspired or directed loans, corporations, and enterprises.

The Entente must remain a loyal supporter and employer of the League of Nations and the Permanent Court of International Justice. Through these channels foreign support may be obtained when needed. Yet the Balkan states must be extremely careful in their support of the League of Nations lest in their zealousness to guard against and control aggression they force out of the League and make enemies of neighbouring and influential states. The peace machinery of the world faces a serious dilemma : if it draws up covenants condemning aggression and then does not punish the aggressor it weakens its influence and prestige. On the other hand, if the members of the League try to act against an aggressor, as they did against Japan, they force out of their membership powerful and necessary members whose support and participation is essential in other situations. The League of Nations is confronted with situations in Europe and Africa not radically different from that which it faced in Asia in 1931, and care need be exercised by the Balkan countries particularly lest they become instrumental in weakening the machinery they hope to strengthen by causing a repetition of 1931-1932, and then lay themselves open to direct action by others.[98]

The discussion of the pan-Balkan movement cannot be concluded without a word concerning the recent French scheme of regional security pacts. The proposed "Eastern Locarno" does not call for the signature of any of the Balkan states, but Rumania and Yugo-

[98] See interesting article "Italy Menaces Europe's Balance," *New York Times*, 30th June, 1935, p. E. 5.

slavia will be indirectly linked to the association by virtue of their alliances with Czechoslovakia, which will be a signatory if the proposal materializes. The Mediterranean pact provides for an alliance of France, Italy, Greece, Turkey, and Yugoslavia. For some reason this agreement is not intended to include Albania or Bulgaria, although it would seem that Albania has as much concern for the Mediterranean as Yugoslavia.

The provisions of these regional security compacts resemble those of the Balkan Pact of Entente. They provide for the continuance of the *status quo* and for collective action against an aggressor. While the conclusion of such treaties may contribute to the *rapprochement* between the Great Powers, it is questionable whether adherence is the best policy for the Balkan states. The Balkan peoples have learned through their own sad experiences in the past the consequences of being tied to the chariot wheels of the Great Powers, and the movement for international organization in the Balkans is designed in large part to free this region from the influence and quarrels of the westerly nations. It is questionable whether the large nations would actively participate in a purely Balkan situation involving a breach of the *status quo,* but they would surely embroil the Balkan states in any development of such a nature in western Europe. However, diplomacy seems to grasp at all such "security" straws, and the Balkan countries will doubtless adhere if the pacts are completed, although there is serious question how their adherence to the Argentine Pact would square with their adherence to such security agreements.

CHAPTER SIX

PEACE OR WAR?

I

ASSASSINATIONS, terrorism, military preparations and mobilizations ! Can there be any question as to the future in such a world ? With a heritage of seven centuries of strife can there be any doubt ? Peace in the Balkans would seem to be an impossible fantasy. Yet an ideal of peace and unity has been conceived and a movement inaugurated to attain its ultimate realization.

Peace in the Balkans, or in any other part of the world, is not to be achieved by the mere conclusion of alliances or compacts condemning or renouncing war. No alliance system, however grand or powerful, has secured permanent peace. While alliances may postpone the day of conflict, they serve to enlarge its arena when hostilities commence and to multiply the rows of inglorious crosses that mar fair fields of grain. And treaties, no matter how solemn and idealistic, are after all still merely written documents, albeit pledges, in the hands of sovereign and reckless states.

The attainment and perfection of a genuine and lasting structure of peace is a more subtle and difficult task. It involves not only the creation of political agreements, but a reconciliation of the economic, social, and intellectual life of the people. The mental and moral barriers erected by fear, propaganda, and history must be broken down and in their stead be substituted the highways of international friendship. The anarchistic implications of the unlimited national sovereignty of the separate states must be compromised in favour of regional organization and government. And this must, in turn, be related to world organization. Also within the Balkan unity, and within the general international organization, there must be personal, civil and political equality. Civil order must be preserved without oppression, and economic endeavour sanctioned but not allowed to precipitate war. Of course no international organization will last for long if it does not make provision for the operation of man's acquisitive instinct ; yet neither will it survive without maintaining control over this activity. How far have the Balkans proceeded in this task of peace-construction ?

Treaty-proofed against war, pledged to peace and co-operation, professing amity and good-will, the Balkans, nevertheless, show all of the surface manifestations of preparation for another war. Frontiers strewn with electrified barbed wire and guarded by machine guns and artillery ; everywhere marching, drilling conscript troops ; railways and roads built only to frontier zones, or locomotives and rolling stock circumspectly turned back at borders ; harassing waits, transfers and inquisitions at frontiers ; hysterical recriminations and vituperations against neighbours in the press ; constantly mounting military expenditures in the face of economic uncertainty ; alliances and military negotiations ! Such is at least the surface panorama of the Balkans today.

The forces conducive to war seem omnipresent. To

the surface ebullitions must be added the more hidden forces. There are the feuds, quarrels, and wars in which the Balkan states were cradled and nurtured which historians and propagandists never permit the peoples to forget. Massacres, conquests, humiliations, deprivations ; each is coloured and tinctured to fit nationalistic prides and prejudices. Together, these memories of the past constitute powerful and insidious obstacles to unity.

The treatment of minorities, national political minorities, as well as alien ethnical, cultural and religious ones, contains the germs of future wars. Discriminations, disfranchisement, cajolings and terrorism wherever practised on such groups in the Balkans or elsewhere render permanent peace uncertain. From them will issue hydra-headed revolts, assassinations, foreign plottings, and propaganda which will ruin efforts at co-operation.

Democracy and peace ; dictatorship and war are not always synonymous. There is no assurance that the adoption of democratic institutions would guarantee peace any more than do the present régimes. In fact, the excesses of democracy in Bulgaria, Greece, and Yugoslavia after the World War brought these countries closer to hostilities than they have been recently. More significant for the preservation of peace than forms of government, are the attitudes and popular tension fostered by those in authority at any given time. Universal military training and partisan propaganda may be instrumental in upholding an edifice of peace, but they may also be productive of headstrong actions in times of emergency, and lead to situations making war inevitable.

In this connection one notes the lack of any outstanding move for disarmament among the Balkans. World disarmament undoubtedly must wait upon agreement between the Great Powers, or else upon absolute guarantees that the territorial integrity of the small states will be respected hereafter by the larger states. Albania, Greece, Rumania, Turkey, and Yugoslavia have due cause — if it is admitted that suspicion and fear based upon historic and current policies may form a basis for such due cause — for keeping a relatively strong military force against extra-Balkan states. However, the presence of such extra-Balkan situations should not entirely vitiate consideration of Balkan limitation of armaments, or the taking of advanced positions in the general disarmament negotiations. No prominent move in these directions is known to have been made in spite of the creeping strangulation of budgets by military and allied expenditures.

The current economic situation in the Balkans is such as to be a more potential force for war than for peace. As has been shown already, the Balkan trade of the six nations constitutes but nine percent of their foreign trade. Far from forming an economic unity or interdependency, the region forms a highly competitive agricultural grouping. No country possesses or has been able to develop any mass production industry, although with the misguided interposition of high tariffs small industries have been stimulated. But here again, there is little diversification, so that wasteful and divisive competition has been increased. Added to this unfortunate situation is the general paucity of intra-Balkan communications, forcing trade outward rather than inward. This is an invitation to the Great Powers to continue that competition and intrigue which has been a source of endless trouble. Continued lackadaisical attitudes toward these economic situations constitute one of the most dangerous phases of Eastern European affairs. The leaders of the Balkan Conferences are quite correct in arguing that durable peace is impossible so long as the territory remains a fertile field for foreign economic concessions and monopolies. Regional planning and the early development of adequate communications would do much to avert or to postpone another war.

The staggering burden of foreign indebtedness is a further menace to peace and independence. Since the middle of the last century the Balkan countries have been a highly absorbent market for foreign investment. In 1930 the foreign indebtedness of Bulgaria amounted to $256,405,000, not counting reparation obligations. The foreign debt of Greece stood at $271,390,000 in the same year, while that of Rumania reached the peak of $917,176,000. The foreign debt of the Republic of Turkey was $473,123,000, and that of Yugoslavia was $564,701,000. These loans have been for (a) industrial purposes ; (b) governmental needs, including the funding of existing indebtedness ; (c) military purchases and expansion ; (d) war requirements, including the payment of indemnities.

Concessions and agreements to purchase certain makes of foreign goods or to employ certain persons have been parts of many of these agreements, with the inevitable result of increased foreign influence and control. It has become almost an axiom in the Balkans that where the loan is there the political alignment is also. International financial supervision has become necessary for five of the states, so burdensome and impossible have become their debt services and so insatiable their demand for new capital. The more recent form of international aid through the League of Nations offers somewhat less political interference than the old system, but will undoubtedly remain a cloak for the policies and direction of the money-lending countries. So long as Britain, Czechoslovakia, France, and Italy continue to be the main sources of loan money their voices will probably be paramount in League financial circles and in the countries indebted to the League. Until the Balkan countries put their economic and political houses in order it will be difficult for them to throw off the financial control of others and with it the dangers of war.

These countries are tied politically to the Big Four in much the same way as they are financially. No one of them is entirely free from connections which would be likely to embroil them in a major war. Rumania and Yugoslavia are, of course, bound directly to Czechoslovakia by the Little Entente, and to France by other agreements. Greece and Turkey are now being pulled into the same orbit through the Balkan Entente which includes Rumania and Yugoslavia, and which pledges the members to concert together on international situations affecting them. Turkey is, moreover, closely related to Russia which in turn is showing increasing evidences of realigning herself with France. Russian alliance to France, plus membership in the Balkan Entente would undoubtedly bring Turkey to the side of Czechoslovakia and France. Albania, willy-nilly, must be reckoned a satellite or tool of Italy. Bulgaria, heretofore leaning toward Germany or Italy, shows some indications of associating herself with the Little Entente and France. So long as there is a minimum of conflict between Britain, Czechoslovakia, France, Germany, and Italy these political relations may be helpful in assuring peace. But conflict among the western nations will almost certainly involve the Balkan states in such hostilities, if not promote them within the peninsula. So long as these countries seek after or accept alliances and associations with the Great Powers for purposes of increasing their own prestige or securing their position against neighbours they must expect to reap the consequences in time of war. "The Balkans may be the powder barrel of Europe," as remarked one delegate to a Balkan Conference, "but the Great Powers have supplied the powder."

II

THE forces which are likely to produce renewed warfare are numerous, powerful, and well organized. In comparison with them the influences making for a stable peace seem ineffective and relatively disorganized. Indeed, the structure of Balkan, as of world peace is loosely built and of few parts. Some of the parts are subject to foreign control, and none of them enjoy the whole-hearted support of the powerful vested interests. However, it would be entirely erroneous to conclude that the maintenance of peace is either impossible or improbable in the Balkans. Peace is sometimes kept in spite of desires and plans and even by those interests seeking war. And while the duration of peace may, on the one hand, promote the intensity of an eventual conflict, it may, on the other hand, provide the opportunity for the consolidation of a structure of peace strong enough to avert the war, or to remove the aggravating causes. Peace, though at moments an uncertain one, has been kept for fifteen years. Few steps, it is true, have been taken until comparatively recently to remove the underlying causes of a new war or to strengthen the existing peace machinery. However, it is gratifying to note that some efforts are now being made in these directions. And it is significant that even though the peace machinery has been severely taxed in some instances by the Balkans, it has held together, solved the immediate problems, and gained the support of the states as a group.

Among the peasantry and statesmen of each nation there is desire for peace. Intangible, largely unorganized and inarticulate, this common reservoir of attitude may be made to form an important force behind the peace movement *if properly controlled and tapped.* The progress made in the reconciliation between Greece and Turkey, and between Bulgaria and Yugoslavia attests to the working of this body of opinion. The readiness of professional and business interests to organize under the aegis of the Balkan Conferences indicates the presence of the same attitude. The net-work of amity, neutrality, and non-aggression treaties, and, latterly the adhesion to the Anti-War Pact also evidence a will to avert another Balkan War. If the codification and implementation of this general desire for peace has proceeded slowly and haltingly, it must not be forgotten that the path is strewn with innumerable pitfalls and fears as already pointed out. It is impossible to believe that all of these manifestations are prevarications and that they will be of no avail whatsoever.

The League of Nations must be regarded as an important part of the Balkan structure of peace. All of the states are members of the League and have given loyal support to its actions. Recourse has been had to the League and to the World Court for the solution of numerous disputes. Three of the states have sought and received financial and economic aid from the League. Twenty disputes of a political nature between or involving Balkan states were submitted to the Council or Assembly for peaceful settlement and conciliation between 1920 and 1933. These constitute a large proportion of the total number of political disputes submitted to the League for such action during these years. In several of these situations mobilizations were proceeding, and in the Bulgar-Greek incident of 1925 hostilities had actually commenced. In all cases involving the Balkans the final conclusions of the League of Nations have been accepted and put into execution, a record not shared by all other disputants who have had their cases considered by this body.

In no locality, other than perhaps Poland, has the post-war minorities problem been more aggravated or tenacious than in the Balkans. Here again, the League of Nations has been of service in clarifying the treaties or in aiding the parties in getting an equitable adjustment of their difficulties. The minorities committee and the Council have dealt successfully with problems involving Albanian and Bulgarian minorities in Greece ; Greek minorities in Bulgaria and Turkey ; and Hungarian minorities in Rumania and Yugoslavia. Less success has been experienced in League efforts concerning the Macedonian situation ; but thanks to the League, the Little Entente, and the Balkan Conferences, the Bulgarians and Yugoslavians have been kept at peace and negotiation so that this situation now promises a better future.

The Balkan states have made liberal use of the Permanent Court of International Justice. Two judgements and five advisory opinions have been handed down by the Court on issues between the Balkan states. And seven judgements and two advisory opinions rendered on cases between a Balkan state and a foreign state. These cases constitute one fourth of the total work of the Court. In all matters the judgements of the Court have been respected by the parties.

This frequent use and loyal support of international organization and law during the last decade and a half is a noteworthy fact. It leads to the hope that a precedent has been established which will be followed in subsequent difficulties. Additional support is lent to this anticipation by the signature and ratification by five states of the "Optional Clause" annexed to the Protocol of Signature of the World Court providing for the compulsory jurisdiction of the Court. Albania, Bulgaria, Greece, Rumania, and Yugoslavia have ratified this clause which gives the Court compulsory jurisdiction over legal disputes with other states, accepting the same obligation, concerning : (a) the interpretation of a treaty ; (b) any question of international law ; (c) the existence of a fact, which, if established, would constitute a breach of an international obligation ; (d) the nature or extent of the reparation to be made for the breach of an international obligation. Bulgaria alone accepted the compulsory jurisdiction unqualifiedly. Albania, Rumania, and Yugoslavia exempted questions which, by international law, fall within their exclusive or domestic jurisdiction. Albania, Greece, and

Rumania exempted from such compulsory jurisdiction disputes relating to their territorial status. The latter two made this specifically include disputes relating to rights of sovereignty over ports and lines of communication, thus clearly indicating an intention to block any Bulgarian efforts to get a Court hearing on the outlets to the sea provided for in the Treaty of Neuilly. Of course, these qualifications cannot permanently block consideration of such a question by the Court, in as much as Article 36 of the Protocol provides, apart from the disputes relating to treaty interpretation specified in paragraph two dealing with compulsory jurisdiction, that the Court shall have jurisdiction over "all matters specifically provided for in treaties and conventions in force." And the Court has indicated plainly enough in numerous cases that if both the parties have ratified its Protocol, and that if it finds that it has jurisdiction, it will proceed to the examination of the merits of the case in spite of the objections of one of the parties. Albania, Greece and Yugoslavia have further exempted from the operation of the compulsory jurisdiction disputes relating to treaties or conventions providing for other methods of pacific settlement.[1]

The success which has attended the work of the League of Nations and the World Court in connection with Balkan disputes demonstrates that the presence of these institutions must be reckoned as one of the most important means of preserving peace in this part of Europe.

The movement toward organization and unity which

[1] Hudson, M. O., *The World Court* 1921-1934, Boston, 1934, pp. 166-184.

has been traced in the preceding chapters must be regarded as the third prop for the structure of peace. Ample evidence has been produced of a willingness to organize along Balkan rather than national lines. For the first time a group consciousness has been developed and local problems have been seen in their proper relation to the general Balkan situation. The Balkan Conferences have sought to lay the foundation for an organization which would (1) provide for common defence against external attack ; (2) reduce the interference of foreign powers ; (3) provide for the presentation of a common front in international affairs ; (4) guarantee peace within the Balkans ; (5) eliminate sterile rivalry ; and (6) level the legal barriers separating the people.

Only the future can tell when the states can and will take over the work and aims of these semi-official Balkan Conferences. In spite of the objections which can be directed at some of the provisions of the Balkan Entente agreements, a commendable step has been taken in the right direction by four of the states. The commitments of the Entente should be helpful in reducing the interference of foreign powers, in providing for a measure of unanimity in international affairs, in preserving peace within the region, and possibly in providing a certain degree of common defence against external attack. But, it is questionable whether a Council composed exclusively of foreign ministers is capable of dealing with economic, social, intellectual, and other technical problems as they should be dealt with to foster ultimate union. A good start has been made on these matters. In view of the excellent ground-work done by the Balkan Conferences, and the success which attended their investigations, it would be a constructive measure if the Entente would urge the continuation of the Conferences and associate them with itself in an advisory capacity. Both the Conferences and the Entente have made valuable contributions to Balkan life, and, as instruments for furthering peace, both should be continued.

III

MUCH remains to be done before peace can be definitely assured even within the peninsula. Only a beginning has been made in fashioning the framework of Balkan organization. Equality and an acceptable system of representation are not yet agreed upon. Machinery for the settlement of disputes is inadequate. Personal and civic rights are not fully protected. Work has just been started on the economic, social, and intellectual problems. But it is of the greatest importance that a serious and intelligent consideration of all these questions has been undertaken.

Here is a movement that is at once significant for the Balkans, for the European political system, and for international organization. It points to an end of internecine war within the peninsula, a removal of many of the causes of European strife, and the creation of *a* Balkan state. It adds incomparable strength to the policies of France and Czechoslovakia. It lays another cornerstone for faith in the effectiveness of international organization and the League of Nations.

Even if the progress of this movement should be temporarily arrested by revolution or even by war, it still remains one of the most unusual and hopeful developments of international affairs.

BIBLIOGRAPHICAL NOTE

To a large extent this study has been based upon material obtainable only in the Balkans, supplemented by information garnered from periodicals and ephemeral sources. Nothing has appeared on the movement in England or the United States, and only one small book in France.

The most important source material is to be found in the bi-monthly *Les Balkans*, published in Athens under the auspices of the Secretariat of the Balkan Conferences. This is the official organ of the movement and has been published continuously since 1932. It contains the resolutions, *voeux*, agenda, speeches, and records of the Conferences and the Councils, as well as articles by interested parties. In addition, it prints most of the miscellaneous documents and reports submitted to the Conferences and Councils by the national groups.

The daily newspaper *Le Messager d'Athènes* is favourably inclined toward the movement and prints much documentary material upon it in advance of *Les Balkans*. It follows the daily developments more completely than any other paper. It also frequently carries articles by leading authorities.

The Near East and India, published fortnightly in London, has regular correspondence from each of the Balkan countries and is much more useful than any of the large foreign daily newspapers, as *Le Temps*, the London *Times*, *Manchester Guardian*, *New York Times*, or *Christian Science Monitor* (Boston). The latter are more inclined to print news of political developments; whereas *The Near East and India* devotes considerable space to non-political events as well. It is especially useful in obtaining news concerning developments and attitudes in the various countries, and gives interesting side-lights on the events, not obtainable in the more official reporter, *Les Balkans*. The paper is avowedly favourable to the movement for union.

Le Mouvement Pacifiste, bi-monthly organ of the Bureau International de la Paix of Geneva, follows the Conferences and Councils and reports their more important actions, but does not contain documentary material.

The League of Nations *Bulletin of Information on the Work of International Organizations* contains incomplete reports of the Conferences and their resolutions. Its usefulness is very limited.

L'Esprit International, Parisian monthly of the Carnegie Endowment for International Peace, has occasional articles on the movement. Those by M. Papanastassiou have been incorporated in his book noted below.

The *Central European Observer* and *L'Europe Central*, both published fortnightly in Prague, are primarily concerned with the Little Entente, but contain some information on the Balkans. Both tend to accentuate the drift of the Balkan Entente into the orbit and policies of the Little Entente. *L'Europe Central*, along with *L'Europe Nouvelle* (Paris), frequently print interesting commentaries by the most informed French authority on the Balkans, M. Albert Mousset.

The British-Bulgarian Review (Sofia), contains sporadic articles on the movement. It is primarily interested in internal economic matters. Its emphasis is pro-Bulgarian.

The *Foreign Policy Association Reports* (New York), occasionally deal with the Balkans. The number entitled "Toward a New Balkan Alignment" (May 9, 1934) throws helpful light on the negotiation of the Pact of Entente.

Much material is published in ephemeral, pamphlet, or mimeographed form, as for instance by the *Agence Anatolie* at Istanbul. Manifestoes are issued by national groups or individuals, but all important material since the first Conference in 1930 has been collected and published, sooner or later, in *Les Balkans*.

BOOKS

A. P. Papanastassiou's *Vers l'Union Balkanique* (Paris, 1934), is by all means the most important work on the movement, not only on account of the close identification of the author with the movement, but also on account of the material which it contains. It traces events from historic times to the signature of the Pact of Entente in the spring of 1934. Its only fault lies in the fact that it is largely a compilation of articles published elsewhere in *Le Messager d'Athènes*, *Les Balkans*, or other periodicals, and as such lacks desirable continuity. It is, however, indispensable.

D. Michev and B. Petkov's *La Fedération Balkanique, origine, développement, et perspectives actuelles* (Sofia, 1930), is useful in following the pre-war ideas of federation and organization. It also deals with the first Conference. It sets forth the Bulgarian point of view.

Arnold Toynbee's annual *Survey of International Affairs* (London), customarily devotes a section to the Balkans. The author's intimate knowledge of international affairs entitles his cautious observations to close attention.

APPENDIX I

ADVANCE PROJECT OF A BALKAN PACT

ADOPTED AT THIRD BALKAN CONFERENCE

Preamble

The III Balkan Conference recognizing the solidarity which unites the Balkan peoples, as well as the necessity of assuring general peace, security and political accord among their States ;

Imbued with the desire of putting in force, in the most complete manner, the system provided for in the Covenant of the League of Nations for the pacific settlement of differences between the Balkan States, of giving additional guarantees of security within the framework of the treaties in force, and of assuring the execution of the provisions of the said treaties, including those concerning the protection of minorities :

Strongly recommends that the respective governments take under consideration the following advance project of a Balkan Pact :

Chapter I

Non-Aggression — Amity

Article 1

Each of the High Contracting Parties engages with the other Contracting Parties not to attack nor invade it, not to have recourse in any case to war against another Contracting Party, but to submit to the methods of pacific settlement in the manner stipulated in the present Pact, all questions of whatever nature they may be which arise to divide them and which it has not been possible to resolve by ordinary diplomatic procedure.

The preceding agreements do not apply to : (1) the exercise of the right of legitimate self-defense; (2) action taken in the application of Article XVI of the Covenant of the League of Nations; and (3) an action resulting from a decision of the Assembly or the Council of the League of Nations, or in the application of Article XV, paragraph 7 of the Covenant of the League of Nations, provided that in the last instance that action is directed against a State which has first been subject to an attack.

Article 2

The Contracting Parties engage to take all necessary measures so that the obligations flowing from the treaties in force may be strictly applied, and in order that a 'spirit of Entente and amity may be cultivated among their peoples.'

CHAPTER II

PACIFIC SETTLEMENT OF DISPUTES

Section I

Conciliation

Article 3

Differences of every sort between two or more Contracting Parties which have not been settled by diplomatic means, with the exception of : (*a*) those relating to the territorial *status quo* of the Contracting Parties and (*b*) those bearing on questions which International Law leaves to the exclusive jurisdiction of States, will be brought before a permanent Conciliation Commission, to be set up within six months after the coming into effect of the present convention.

Article 4

The permanent Conciliation Commission will be made up of representatives of the Contracting Parties. Each Contracting Party may not have more than two representatives nor more than one vote. It will always and at once replace the representatives named by it.

Article 5

The functions of the President of the Commission will be exercised in turn and in alphabetical order among the Contracting Parties, by one of the representatives of each State member of the Commission. The duration of the office is one year.

Article 6

The Commission will meet on a request addressed to the President by either of the disputing Parties.

The request, after having set forth briefly the object of the dispute, will contain an invitation to the Commission to take all measures proper for a conciliation.

Article 7

The Commission will convene at whatever place is designated by the President. That place must be in the territory of one of the Parties, unless the Commission decides otherwise.

Article 8

The work of the Conciliation Commission will be public only after a decision of the Commission and with the assent of the disputing Parties.

Article 9

The Commission will determine its own rules of procedure. In matters of inquiry, the Commission, if it has not unanimously decided otherwise, will conform to the provisions of Title III of the Hague Convention of Oct. 18, 1907, for the pacific settlement of international disputes.

Article 10

The disputing Parties will be represented before the Commission by agents having the mission of serving as intermediaries between the Parties and the Commission; they may be assisted by counsel or experts named by them, and they may demand a hearing for all persons whose testimony may seem useful to them.

Article 11

The Commission will have, on its part, the right to demand oral explanations by the agents, counsel, and experts of the two Parties, as well as by any persons whom it may judge useful to cause to appear with the consent of their governments.

Article 12

The decisions of the Commission will be taken by a majority of the members present at the session.

In case of a tie, the President casts the deciding vote. That rule does not apply when the Commission is required to pronounce on the arrangements proposed in Article 15, paragraph 1.

Article 13

The Parties undertake to facilitate the work of the Commission of Conciliation, and in particular to furnish it in the greatest possible measure with all documents and useful information, as well as to employ all means at their disposal to permit it to travel in their territory and according to their law to the examination and hearing of witnesses or experts, and to transportation on their lines.

Article 14

The expenses incurred by the functioning of the Commission will be equally borne by the Contracting Parties.

Article 15

The Commission in order to clear up the questions in dispute will have the right to obtain, by inquiry or otherwise, all information useful for conciliating the Parties. The Commission, after examining the affair, will reveal to the Parties the terms which appear to it to be suitable for settlement.

At the end of its work, the Commission will draw up a statement setting forth the case, whether the Parties have arranged the affair, and if possible the conditions of settlement, or whether it has not been possible to conciliate the Parties. The statement will not reveal whether the decisions of the Commission have been reached by majority or unanimous vote.

The work of the Commission must be completed within six months of the time it is seized of the case, unless the Parties agree to a longer time.

Article 16

The decision of the Commission will be communicated to the Parties with the least possible delay. It remains with the Parties to decide upon the publication of the report.

SECTION II

JUDICIAL OR ARBITRAL SETTLEMENT

Article 17

If within the month following the communication of the decision of the Commission to the disputing Parties, they are not satisfied, the differences will be submitted, at the request of one of the Parties, to the Permanent Court of International Justice, unless the Parties agree to submit them to an arbitration tribunal.

Article 18

If the Parties agree to have recourse to arbitration, they will draw up a compromis for submission.

In default of agreement upon a compromis, or failing the designation of arbiters or the functioning of the court for any reason whatsoever, and after an interval of three months, each Party has the right to appeal directly to the Permanent Court of International Justice.

CHAPTER III

MUTUAL ASSISTANCE

Article 19

If one of the High Contracting Parties believes that a violation of the agreement of non-aggression contained in Article I of the present treaty has been committed, it will submit the matter at once to the Council of the League of Nations.

If the Council of the League of Nations finds, by a vote of 4/5ths of the members, the disputing Parties excluded, that a violation has been committed, it will immediately advise the Powers signatory of the present agreement, and each of them engages to go immediately to the assistance of the Power against which the unlawful action has been directed.

Article 20

In the event of a flagrant violation of the engagement of non-aggression by one of the High Contracting Parties, each of the other High Contracting Parties hereby agree to go at once to the aid of the Party against which such a violation or contravention has been directed, after the said Power has proven that the violation constitutes an unprovoked act of aggression and that as a result of the crossing of the frontiers, or of the opening of hostilities, an immediate action is necessary. Nevertheless, the Council of the League of Nations seized of the question, and conforming to the first paragraph of the preceding article, will make known the results of its deliberations. The High Contracting Parties agree in any case to act in conformity with a recommendation made by 4/5ths vote of the Council, the disputing Parties votes not being counted.

Chapter IV

Protection of Minorities

Article 21

In order to render more effective the protection of minorities, the Contracting Parties, on the basis of the respective clauses of the treaties concerning minorities, which continue to produce their effects, take the following obligations :

Article 22

Each Contracting Party will create a Minorities Office to which will be addressed petitions concerning the application of the minorities treaties.

Article 23

The Contracting Parties will proceed to the creation of an Inter-Balkan Minorities Commission, which will be composed of six members, one from each State, and which will sit in turn each year in each of the signatory States.

Article 24

The Commission will establish its own rules of procedure.

At the request of the above mentioned Commission, the Minorities Offices will submit to it the petitions addressed to them, and will communicate to it the orders made as well as the results obtained. After the examination of each affair, the Commission will issue its decision.

Article 25

(*a*) The Contracting States undertake to conform to all recommendations unanimously adopted by the Commission :

(*b*) In case of difference of opinion within the Commission, the latter will transmit the documents concerning the affair to the Secretariat of the League of Nations if the petitioner, making use of the machinery provided in the minorities treaties, has addressed a petition at the same time to the Secretariat of the League of Nations.

Article 26

The petitions concerning the protection of minorities must represent the free will of the interested parties. The minorities must conduct themselves in a loyal fashion toward the State in whose territory they are living and abstain from all action directed against the State.

The contracting Parties agree to take all necessary measures to prevent any action likely to trouble the peace and good relations between the Balkan peoples.

CHAPTER V

GENERAL PROVISIONS

Article 27

Differences for the solution of which a special procedure may be provided by other conventions in force between the Contracting Parties will be regulated in conformity with the terms of those conventions.

The present Pact does not affect agreements in force establishing for the Contracting Parties a conciliation procedure or, in matters of arbitration or judicial settlement, engagements assuring the solution of differences. However, if the accords provide only a conciliation procedure, after the exhaustion of that procedure, the provisions of the present Treaty relative to judicial or arbitral settlement will be applied.

Article 28

If the Conciliation Commission finds itself seized by one of the Contracting Parties of a difference which the other Party in dispute acting on the conventions in force has carried to the Permanent Court of International Justice or an arbitration tribunal, the Commission will suspend the examination of the differences until the court or tribunal may have decided on the question of jurisdiction. It will be the same if the court or tribunal has been appealed to by one of the Parties in the course of conciliation procedure.

Article 29

If a difference arises whose object, according to the domestic laws of one of the Parties, calls into account the competence of judicial or administrative authorities, the other Party may demand that that dispute be submitted to the different procedures provided for in the Present Treaty, if a definite decision has not been rendered within a reasonable time by the competent authority.

The Party which in this case wishes to have recourse to the procedure provided for in the present Pact must notify its intention to the other Party within one year of the time in which the objected decision has been rendered.

Article 30

If the judicial or arbitral sentence declares that a decision made or measure ordered by an authority of one of the Parties is partly or entirely in opposition to international law, and if the constitutional law of the said Party does not permit or would only partially permit the erasure of the consequences of that decision or action, it is agreed that there shall be accorded to the injured party an equitable satisfaction by the arbitral or judicial sentence.

Article 31

In every case where a dispute becomes the object of an arbitral or judicial settlement, especially if the question on the subject of which the Parties are divided results from acts already committed or on the point of being committed, the Permanent Court of International Justice, sitting in conformity with article 41 of its Statute, or the arbitral tribunal, will indicate in the shortest possible time what provisional measures shall be taken. The Parties in dispute are bound to conform thereby.

If the Conciliation Commission finds itself with the dispute, it will recommend to the Parties the provisional measures which it deems useful.

The Contracting Parties agree to refrain from acts likely to have an effect prejudicial to the execution of the arbitral or judicial decision, or to the arrangements proposed by the conciliation Commission and, in general, to avoid any act of whatever nature, likely to aggravate or extend the dispute.

Article 32

The present Convention will be applicable between the Contracting Powers even when a third Power may have an interest in the dispute.

In the conciliation procedure, the contesting States may, as a result of agreement, invite the presence of a third State.

In the judicial or arbitral procedure, if a third State considers that it has a legal interest in a dispute, it may address a request for intervention to the Permanent Court of International Justice or to an arbitral tribunal.

Article 33

When a dispute arises from the interpretation of a convention in which States other than the disputants have participated, the Bureau of the Permanent Court of International Justice, or the arbitral tribunal shall advise them without delay.

Each of them will have the right to intervene in the litigation, and if any State exercises that right, the interpretation in the decision will be binding upon them.

Article 34

Differences relative to the interpretation or application of the present Pact, save those mentioned in Article 3, paragraph (a) shall be submitted to the Permanent Court of International Justice.

Article 35

In case a dispute should arise between more than two of the Contracting Parties, it shall be subject to the judicial procedure set forth in the Statute of the Permanent Court of International Justice.

Article 36

Nothing in the present Pact shall be interpreted as interfering with the duty of the League of Nations to take, at any moment, proper measures for safeguarding the peace of the world.

Nothing in the present Agreement shall be interpreted as interfering with the obligations imposed upon the Contracting Parties who are members of the League of Nations by the Covenant of the League of Nations.

Article 37

The present Pact shall come into force ninety days following the receipt by the Secretary General of the League of Nations of the ratifications of at least four Contracting Parties.

Article 38

The present treaty shall be ratified and the ratifications shall be deposited at . . . It will be registered with the Secretariat of the League of Nations.

Article 39

The following conventions are abrogated by the present agreement . . . (the different conventions of arbitration, conciliation, etc., existing between the Balkan States and which, by the signature of the present treaty have become superfluous.)

In faith whereof the undersigned plenipotentiaries have signed the Present Pact. . .[1]

[1] Papanastassiou, *op. cit.*, pp. 245-257. Unofficial translation.

APPENDIX II

GENERAL ACT OF CONCILIATION, ARBITRATION AND JUDICIAL SETTLEMENT BETWEEN THE STATES OF THE LITTLE ENTENTE

THE PRESIDENT OF THE CZECHOSLOVAK REPUBLIC, HIS MAJESTY THE KING OF RUMANIA, AND HIS MAJESTY THE KING OF THE SERBS, CROATS, AND SLOVENES,

Inspired by the friendly relations existing between their respective nations and imbued with the spirit of confident cordiality which characterises their reciprocal intercourse ;

Sincerely desirous of ensuring, by pacific means, the settlement of any disputes which may arise between their countries ;

Noting that respect for the rights established by treaties or arising out of international law is binding upon international courts ;

Recognising that the rights of each State cannot be modified without its consent ;

Considering that the faithful observance, under the auspices of the League of Nations, of methods of pacific procedure will permit of the settlement of all international disputes ;

Highly appreciating the recommendation made to all States by the Assembly of the League of Nations, in its resolution of September 26th, 1928, to conclude conventions for the pacific settlement of international disputes ;

Having resolved to give effect to their common intention in a Convention, and with that object have appointed as their Plenipotentiaries :

THE PRESIDENT OF THE CZECHOSLOVAK REPUBLIC
His Excellency Dr. Eduard Benes, Minister for Foreign
Affairs of the Czechoslovak Republic ;

HIS MAJESTY THE KING OF RUMANIA :
His Excellency Monsieur George Mironescu, Minister for
Foreign Affairs of the Kingdom of Rumania ;

HIS MAJESTY THE KING OF THE SERBS, CROATS, AND
SLOVENES :
His Excellency Monsieur Kosta Kumanudi, Doctor of
Law and Acting Minister for Foreign Affairs of the
Kingdom of the Serbs, Croats, and Slovenes ;

Who, having deposited their full powers, found in good
and due form have agreed on the following provisions :

CHAPTER I

PACIFIC SETTLEMENT IN GENERAL

Article 1

Disputes of every kind which may arise between the High
Contracting Parties, or between two of them, and which it has
not been possible to settle by diplomacy shall be submitted, under
the conditions laid down in the present Convention, for settlement by judicial means or arbitration, preceded, according to
circumstances, as a compulsory or optional measure, by recourse
to the procedure of conciliation.

This provision does not apply to disputes arising out of events
prior to the present Convention and belonging to the past, or to
disputes relating to questions which, according to international
law, fall within the sole competence of the States.

Article 2

1. Disputes for the settlement of which a special procedure is
laid down in other conventions in force between the High Contracting Parties shall be settled in conformity with the provisions
of those conventions.

2. The present Convention shall not affect any agreements in force by which conciliation procedure is established between the High Contracting Parties or by which the High Contracting Parties have assumed obligations to resort to arbitration or judicial settlement for the purpose of settling the dispute. If, however, these agreements provide only for a procedure of conciliation, the provisions of the present Convention concerning judicial settlement or arbitration shall be applied after such procedure has been followed without result.

Article 3

1. In the case of a dispute the occasion of which, according to the municipal law of one of the High Contracting Parties, falls within the competence of the judicial authorities, the Party in question may object to the dispute being submitted for settlement by the various procedures laid down in the present Convention.

2. A dispute which falls within the competence of the administrative authorities may not be submitted for settlement by the various procedures laid down in the present Convention until a final decision has been pronounced, within a reasonable time, by the competent authority.

In such case, the Party which desires to resort to the procedures laid down in the present Convention must notify the other Party of its intention within a period of one year from the date of the aforementioned decision.

CHAPTER II

JUDICIAL SETTLEMENT

Article 4

All disputes with regard to which the Parties are in conflict as to their respective rights shall be submitted for decision to the Permanent Court of International Justice, unless the Parties agree, in the manner hereinafter provided, to have resort to an arbitral tribunal.

It is understood that the disputes referred to above include in particular those mentioned in Article 36 of the Statute of the Permanent Court of International Justice.

Article 5

If the Parties agree to submit the disputes mentioned in the preceding article to an arbitral tribunal, they shall draw up a special agreement in which they shall specify the subject of the dispute, the selection of the arbitrators and the procedure to be followed. In the absence of sufficient particulars in the special agreement, the provisions of the Hague Convention of October 18th, 1907, for the Pacific Settlement of International Disputes, shall apply so far as is necessary. If nothing is laid down in the special agreement as to the rules regarding the substance of the dispute to be followed by the arbitrators, the tribunal shall apply the substantive rules enumerated in Article 38 of the Statute of the Permanent Court of International Justice.

Article 6

If the Parties fail to agree concerning the special agreement referred to in the preceding article, or fail to appoint arbitrators, either Party shall be at liberty, after giving three months' notice, to bring the dispute by an application direct before the Permanent Court of International Justice.

Article 7

1. In the case of the dispute mentioned in Article 4, before any procedure before the Permanent Court of International Justice or any arbitral tribunal, the Parties may agree to have recourse to the conciliation procedure provided for in the present Convention.

2. In the event of recourse to and failure of conciliation, neither Party may bring the dispute before the Permanent Court of International Justice or call for the constitution of the arbitral tribunal referred to in Article 5 before the expiration of one month from the termination of the proceedings of the Conciliation Commission.

Chapter III

Conciliation

Article 8

All disputes between the parties other than the disputes mentioned in Article 4 shall be submitted obligatorily to a procedure of conciliation before they can form the subject of a settlement by arbitration.

Article 9

The disputes referred to in the preceding article shall be submitted to a permanent or special Conciliation Commission constituted by the High Contracting Parties.

Article 10

On a request to that effect being made by one of the Contracting Parties to the other Party, a permanent Conciliation Commission shall be constituted within a period of six months.

Article 11

Unless the parties agree otherwise, the Conciliation Commission shall be constituted as follows :

1. The Commission shall be composed of five members. The Parties shall each nominate one commissioner, who may be chosen from among their respective nationals. The three other commissioners shall be appointed by agreement from among the nationals of third Powers. These three commissioners must be of different nationalities and must not be habitually resident in the territory nor be in the service of the Parties concerned. The High Contracting Parties shall appoint the President of the Commission from among their number.

2. The commissioners shall be appointed for three years. They shall be re-eligible. The commissioners appointed jointly may be replaced during the course of their mandate by agreement between the Parties. Any one of the High Contracting Parties may, however, at any time replace the commissioner whom it has appointed. Even if replaced, the commissioners shall

continue to exercise their functions until the termination of the work in hand.

3. Vacancies which may occur as a result of death, resignation or any other cause shall be filled within the shortest possible time in the manner fixed for the nominations.

Article 12

If, when a dispute arises, no permanent Conciliation Commission appointed by the Parties is in existence, a special commission shall be constituted for the examination of the dispute within a period of three months from the date on which a request to that effect is made by one of the Parties to the other Party. The necessary appointments shall be made in the manner laid down in the preceding article, unless the Parties decide otherwise.

Article 13

1. If the appointment of the commissioners to be designated jointly is not made within the periods provided for in Articles 10 and 12, the making of the necessary appointments shall be entrusted to a third Power, chosen by agreement between the Parties or, on request of the Parties, to the Council of the League of Nations.

2. If no agreement is reached on either of these procedures, each Party shall designate a different Power and the appointments shall be made jointly by the Powers thus chosen.

3. If, within a period of three months, these two Powers have been unable to reach an agreement, each of them shall submit a number of candidates equal to the number of members to be appointed. It shall then be decided by lot which of the candidates thus designated shall be appointed.

Article 14

1. Disputes shall be brought before the Conciliation Commission by means of an application addressed to the President of the two Parties acting in agreement, or, in default thereof, by one or other of the Parties.

2. The application, after giving a summary account of the subject of the dispute, shall contain the invitation to the Com-

mission to take all necessary steps with a view to arriving at an amicable solution.

3. If the application emanates from only one of the Parties, the other Party shall without delay be notified by it.

Article 15

1. Within fifteen days from the date on which a dispute has been brought by one of the Parties before a permanent Conciliation Commission, any Party may replace its own commissioner, for the examination of the particular dispute, by a person possessing special competence in the matter.

2. The Party making use of this right shall immediately notify the other Party ; the latter shall in such case be entitled to take similar action within fifteen days from the date on which it received the notification.

Article 16

In the absence of agreement to the contrary between the Parties, the Conciliation Commission shall meet at a place selected by its President.

Article 17

The work of the Conciliation Commission shall not be conducted in public unless a decision to that effect is taken by the Commission with the consent of the Parties.

Article 18

1. In the absence of agreement to the contrary between the Parties, the Conciliation Commission shall lay down its own procedure, which in any case must provide for the Parties being heard. In regard to enquiries, the Commission, unless it decided unanimously to the contrary, shall act in accordance with the provisions of Part III of the Hague Convention of October 18th, 1907, for the Pacific Settlement of International Disputes.

2. The Parties shall be represented before the Conciliation Commission by agents, whose duty shall be to act as intermediaries between them and the Commission. They may, moreover, be assisted by counsel and experts appointed by them for that pur-

pose and may request that all persons whose evidence appears to them desirable shall be heard.

3. The Commission, for its part, shall be entitled to request oral explanations from the agents, counsel and experts of both Parties, as well as from all persons it may think desirable to summon with the consent of their Governments.

Article 19

In the absence of agreement to the contrary between the Parties, decisions of the Conciliation Commission shall be taken by a majority vote, and the Commission may only take decisions on the substance of the dispute if all its members are present.

Article 20

The High Contracting Parties undertake to facilitate the work of the Conciliation Commission, and in particular to supply it to the greatest possible extent with all relevant documents and information, as well as to use the means at their disposal to allow it to proceed in their territory, and in accordance with their law, to the summoning and hearing of witnesses or experts and to visit the localities in question.

Article 21

1. During the proceedings of the Commission, each of the commissioners shall receive emoluments the amount of which shall be fixed by agreement between the Parties, each of which shall contribute an equal share.

2. The general expenses arising out of the working of the Commission shall be divided in the same manner.

Article 22

1. The task of the Conciliation Commission shall be to elucidate the questions in dispute, to collect with that object all necessary information by means of enquiry or otherwise, and to endeavour to bring the Parties to an agreement. It may, after the case has been examined, inform the Parties of the terms of settlement which seem suitable to it, and lay down the period within which they are to make their decision.

2. At the close of its proceedings, the Commission shall draw up a procès-verbal stating, as the case may be, either that the Parties have come to an agreement, and, if need arises, the terms of the agreement, or that it has been impossible to effect a settlement. No mention shall be made in the procès-verbal as to whether the Commission's decisions were taken unanimously or by a majority vote.

3. The proceedings of the Commission must, unless the Parties agree otherwise, be terminated within six months from the date on which the Commission shall have been given cognisance of the dispute.

Article 23

The Commission's procès-verbal shall be communicated without delay to the Parties. The Parties shall decide whether it shall be published.

Chapter IV

Settlement by Arbitration

Article 24

If the Parties have not reached an agreement within a month from the termination of the proceedings of the Conciliation Commission mentioned in the previous articles, the question shall be brought before an arbitral tribunal which, unless the Parties agree otherwise, shall be constituted in the manner indicated below.

Should, however, both Parties agree, the question may, if it is a political one, be submitted to the Council of the League of Nations, which shall decide in accordance with Article 15 of the Covenant.

Article 25

The arbitral tribunal shall consist of five members. The Parties shall each nominate one member, who may be chosen from among their respective nationals. The other two arbitrators and the umpire shall be chosen by agreement from among the nationals of third Powers. They must be of different nationalities, and must not be habitually resident in the territory or be in the service of the Parties concerned.

Article 26

1. If the appointment of the members of the arbitral tribunal is not made within a period of three months from the date on which one of the Parties requested the other Party to constitute an arbitral tribunal, a third Power, chosen by agreement between the Parties, shall be requested to make the necessary appointments.

2. If no agreement is reached on this point, each Party shall designate a different Power, and the appointments shall be made jointly by the Powers thus chosen.

3. If within a period of three months the Powers so chosen have been unable to reach an agreement, the necessary appointments shall be made by the President of the Permanent Court of International Justice. If the latter is prevented from acting or if he is a national of one of the Parties, the appointments shall be made by the Vice-President. If the latter is prevented from acting or if he is a national of one of the Parties, the appointments shall be made by the oldest member of the Court who is not a national of either Party.

Article 27

Vacancies which may occur as a result of death, resignation or other cause shall be filled within the shortest possible time in the manner fixed for the nominations.

Article 28

The Parties shall draw up a special agreement determining the subject of the dispute and the details of the procedure.

Article 29

In the absence of sufficient particulars in the special agreement regarding the matters referred to in the preceding article, the provisions of the Hague Convention of October 18th, 1907 for the Pacific Settlement of International Disputes shall apply so far as is necessary.

Article 30

Failing the conclusion of a special agreement within a period of three months from the date on which the tribunal is constituted, the dispute may be brought before the tribunal by an application from one or the other Party.

Article 31

If nothing is laid down in the special agreement or no special agreement has been made, the tribunal shall apply the rules in regard to the substance of the dispute enumerated in Article 38 of the Statute of the Permanent Court of International Justice. In so far as there exist no such rules applicable to the dispute, the tribunal shall decide *ex aequo et bono*.

CHAPTER V

DISPUTES BETWEEN THE THREE CONTRACTING PARTIES

Article 32

Should a dispute arise between all the High Contracting Parties, the following rules shall be observed with regard to the procedures described in the foregoing provisions:

As regards conciliation procedure, a special commission shall always be set up. The composition of the commission shall vary according to whether all the Parties have separate interests, or two of them act conjointly.

In the former case, the Parties shall each appoint one commissioner, and shall jointly appoint commissioners, nationals of third Powers, who shall number one more than the commissioners appointed separately by the Parties.

In the latter case, the Parties acting conjointly shall agree to appoint their own commissioner jointly, and at the same time agree with the other Party as regards the appointment of the commissioners chosen from among the nationals of third Powers.

In either case the Parties shall, unless they agree otherwise, apply Articles 12 et seq. of the present Convention in so far as these are compatible with the provisions of the present article.

As regards judicial procedure, the Statute of the Permanent Court of International Justice shall apply.

As regards arbitration, if the Parties fail to agree on the composition of the tribunal, any Party may, in the case of disputes referred to in Article 4, bring the dispute by an application direct before the Permanent Court of International Justice ; in the case of disputes referred to in Article 8, Articles 25 et seq. shall apply, but each of the Parties which has separate interests shall appoint one arbitrator and the arbitrators appointed separately by the Parties shall always number one less than the other arbitrators.

CHAPTER VI

GENERAL PROVISIONS

Article 33

1. In all cases where a dispute forms the object of arbitration or judicial proceedings, and in particular if the question on which the Parties differ arises out of acts already committed or on the point of being committed, the Permanent Court of International Justice, acting in accordance with Article 41 of its Statute, or the arbitral tribunal, shall lay down within the shortest possible time the provisional measures to be adopted. The Parties shall be bound to comply with such measures.

2. If the dispute is brought before a Conciliation Commission, the latter may recommend to the Parties the adoption of such provisional measures as it considers suitable.

3. The Parties undertake to abstain from all measures likely to react prejudicially on the execution of the judicial decision or arbitral award or on the arrangements proposed by the Conciliation Commission, and, in general, to abstain from any act whatsoever which might aggravate or extend the dispute.

Article 34

If in the judicial decision or arbitral award it is declared that a judgment or measure enjoined by a court of law or any other authority of one of the Parties to the dispute is wholly or partly contrary to international law, and if the constitutional law of that Party does not allow or only imperfectly allows of the consequences of the judgment or measure in question being annulled, the Parties agree that the judicial decision or arbitral award shall grant the injured Party equitable satisfaction.

Article 35

1. The present Convention shall be applicable as between the High Contracting Parties, even though a third Power has an interest in the dispute.

2. In conciliation procedure, the Parties may agree to invite such third Power to intervene.

3. In judicial procedure or arbitration, if a third Power should consider that it has an interest of a legal nature which may be affected by the decision in the case, it may submit to the Permanent Court of International Justice or to the arbitral tribunal a request to intervene as a third party.

It will be for the Court or the tribunal to decide upon this request.

4. Whenever the question is one relating to the interpretation of a Convention to which States other than those concerned in the case are Parties, the Registrar of the Permanent Court of International Justice or the arbitral tribunal shall notify all such States forthwith.

Every State so notified has the right to intervene in the proceedings, but if it uses this right, the interpretation given in the decision shall be binding upon it.

Article 36

Disputes relating to the interpretation or the application of the present Convention, including those concerning the classification of disputes, shall be submitted to the Permanent Court of International Justice.

Article 37

The present Convention, which is in conformity with the Covenant of the League of Nations, shall not be interpreted as restricting the duty of the League to take at any time, whatever action may be deemed wise and effectual to safeguard the peace of the world.

Article 38

1. The present Convention shall be ratified and the instruments of ratification shall be exchanged at Bucharest.

It shall be registered with the Secretariat of the League of Nations.

2. The present Convention shall remain in force for a period of five years from the date of the exchange of ratifications.

3. Unless denounced at least six months before the expiration of this period, it shall remain in force for a further period of five years, and similarly thereafter.

4. Notwithstanding denunciation by one of the Contracting Parties, all proceedings pending at the expiration of the current period of the Convention shall be duly completed.

In Faith Whereof the above-mentioned Plenipotentiaries have signed the present Convention.

Done at Belgrade in triplicate on May 21st, one thousand nine hundred and twenty-nine.

(L.S.) Dr. Edward Benes
(L.S.) G. G. Mironescu
(L.S.) Dr. K. Kumanudi [1]

[1] League of Nations, *Treaty Series,* Vol. XCVI, pp. 311-331.

APPENDIX III

THE LITTLE ENTENTE TREATIES OF ALLIANCE

I. CONVENTION OF ALLIANCE BETWEEN THE KINGDOM OF THE SERBS, CROATS, AND SLOVENES AND THE CZECHOSLOVAK REPUBLIC, SIGNED AT BELGRADE ON THE 14TH AUGUST, 1920.

Firmly resolved to maintain the Peace obtained by so many sacrifices, and provided for by the Covenant of the League of Nations, as well as the situation created by the Treaty concluded at Trianon on June 4, 1920, between the Allied and Associated Powers on the one hand, and Hungary on the other, the President of the Czechoslovak Republic and His Majesty the King of the Serbs, Croats, and Slovenes have agreed to conclude a Defensive Convention ... (and the signatories) have agreed as follows :

Article 1

In case of an unprovoked attack on the part of Hungary against one of the High Contracting Parties, the other Party agrees to assist in the defence of the Party attacked, in the manner laid down by the arrangement provided for in Article 2 of the present Convention.

Article 2

The competent Technical Authorities of the Czechoslovak Republic and the Kingdom of the Serbs, Croats, and Slovenes shall decide, by mutual agreement, upon the provisions necessary for the execution of the present Convention.

Article 3

Neither of the High Contracting Parties shall conclude an

alliance with a third Power without preliminary notice to the other.

Article 4

The present Convention shall be valid for two years from the date of the exchange of ratifications. On the expiration of this period, each of the Contracting Parties shall have the option of denouncing the present Convention. It shall, however, remain in force for six months after the date of denunciation.

* * * * *

II. Convention of Alliance Between the Kingdom of Rumania and the Czechoslovak Republic, Signed at Bucharest on the 23rd April, 1921.

Firmly resolved to maintain the peace obtained by so many sacrifices, and provided for by the Covenant of the League of Nations, as well as the situation created by the Treaty concluded at Trianon on June 4, 1920, between the Allied and Associated Powers on the one hand, and Hungary on the other, the President of the Czechoslovak Republic and His Majesty the King of Rumania, have agreed to conclude a Defensive Convention ... (and the signatories) have agreed as follows :

Article 1

In case of an unprovoked attack on the part of Hungary against one of the High Contracting Parties, the other Party agrees to assist in the defence of the party attacked, in the manner laid down by the arrangement provided for in Article 2 of the present Convention.

Article 2

The competent Technical Authorities of the Czechoslovak Republic and Rumania shall decide by mutual agreement and in a Military Convention to be concluded, upon the provisions necessary for the execution of the present Convention.

Article 3

Neither of the High Contracting Parties shall conclude an

alliance with a third Power without preliminary notice to the other.

Article 4

For the purpose of co-ordinating their efforts to maintain peace, the two Governments undertake to consult together on questions of foreign policy concerning their relations with Hungary.

Article 5

The present Convention shall be valid for two years from the date of the exchange of ratifications. On the expiration of this period each of the Contracting Parties shall have the option of denouncing the present Convention. It shall, however, remain in force for six months after the date of denunciation.

* * * * *

III. CONVENTION OF DEFENSIVE ALLIANCE BETWEEN RUMANIA AND THE KINGDOM OF THE SERBS, CROATS, AND SLOVENES, SIGNED AT BELGRADE, 7TH JUNE, 1921.

Firmly resolved to maintain the peace obtained by so many sacrifices and the situation created by the Treaty concluded at Trianon on June 4, 1920, between the Allied and Associated Powers, of the one part, and Hungary, of the other part, and by the Treaty of Neuilly-sur-Seine, concluded on November 27, 1919, between the Allied and Associated Powers, of the one part, and Bulgaria, of the other part, His Majesty the King of Rumania and His Majesty the King of the Serbs, Croats, and Slovenes have agreed to conclude a Defensive Convention ... (and the signatories) have agreed as follows :

Article 1

In case of an unprovoked attack on the part of Hungary or of Bulgaria or of both these Powers against one of the High Contracting Parties with the object of subverting the situation created by the Treaty of Peace concluded at Trianon, or by that concluded at Neuilly-sur-Seine, the other Party agrees to assist in the defence of the Party attacked in the manner laid down by the arrangement provided for in Article 2 of the present Convention.

Article 2

The competent technical authorities of Rumania and of the Kingdom of Serbs, Croats, and Slovenes shall by mutual agreement determine in a military Convention to be concluded as soon as possible, the provisions necessary for the execution of the present Convention.

Article 3

Neither of the High Contracting Parties shall conclude an alliance with a third Power without first giving notice to the other.

Article 4

For the purpose of co-ordinating their efforts to maintain peace, the two Governments undertake to consult together on questions of foreign policy concerning their relations with Hungary and Bulgaria.

Article 5

The present Convention shall be valid for two years from the date of the exchange of ratifications. On the expiration of this period each of the Contracting Parties shall have the right to denounce the present Convention. It shall, however, remain in force for six months after the date of denunciation.

* * * * *

IV. Treaty of Alliance Between the Kingdom of the Serbs, Croats, and Slovenes and the Czechoslovak Republic, Signed at Marianske Lazne, 31st August, 1922.

The Governments of the Kingdom of the Serbs, Croats, and Slovenes, and the Czechoslovak Republic desirous of prolonging and completing the Agreement concluded between them on August 14, 1920, by new provisions having the following objects :

(*a*) the strengthening and maintenance of peace ;
(*b*) the consolidation and extension of the political and economic bonds between the two States,

have accepted, by common agreement, the following Articles . . . (and the signatories) have agreed as follows :

Article 1

The Agreement concluded at Belgrade, on August 14, 1920, between the Kingdom of the Serbs, Croats, and Slovenes and the Czechoslovak Republic is prolonged for the duration of the present Convention.

Article 2

The High Contracting Parties take note of the political and military treaties and of the agreements concluded between the Czechoslovak Republic and Rumania, Austria and Poland on the one hand, and of the similar agreements concluded between the Kingdom of the Serbs, Croats, and Slovenes, and Rumania and Italy on the other hand.

Article 3

The High Contracting Parties will endeavour to establish on a solid foundation all their economic, financial and transport relations and mutually to ensure the closest co-operation in these relations ; for this purpose they will conclude arrangements on these subjects and particularly a commercial treaty for this purpose.

Article 4

The two High Contracting Parties undertake to give each other in general all possible political and diplomatic support in their international relations ; should they consider their common interests to be threatened, they undertake to consider together steps for their protection.

Article 5

The proper authorities of the Kingdom of the Serbs, Croats, and Slovenes and the Czechoslovak Republic shall come to a mutual understanding with a view to taking all the steps necessary for the application of the present Convention.

Article 6

The present Convention shall remain in force for five years from the date on which the instruments of ratification are exchanged.

At the expiration of these five years either of the High Contracting Parties shall be free to denounce the present Convention giving six months' previous notice to the other party.[1]

---

[1] League of Nations, *Treaty Series*, Vol. VI, pp. 209-219 ; *ibid.*, Vol. XIII, pp. 231-235 ; *ibid.*, Vol. LIV, pp. 257-261. These alliance treaties were prolonged for indefinite five year periods, unless denounced, by Protocols concluded 21st May, 1929. League of Nations, *Treaty Series*, Vol. XCIV, p. 53 ; *ibid.*, Vol. XCVI, p. 309.

APPENDIX IV

STATUTE OF THE BALKAN ENTENTE

The States signatories of the Balkan Entente desirous of maintaining and organizing peace, being firmly resolved to intensify economic relations with all States without distinction and between the signatories of the Balkan Entente in particular,

Have decided to give to the relations of amity and alliance which exist between the four States of the Balkan Entente an organized and stable base.

Are convinced of the necessity of realizing that stability by the establishment of a directive organ for their common policy.

Have resolved to confirm the practice of their common work realized since the signature of the Balkan Entente Pact and to provide for the future as follows:

1. A permanent Council of the States of the Balkan Entente composed of the Ministers of Foreign Affairs of the respective countries is constituted as a directive organ for the common policy of the group of four States. The decisions of the Council must be unanimous.

2. The permanent Council, in addition to the regular relations by diplomatic means shall meet at least twice a year. The annual required meetings shall take place in turn in each of the four States.

If necessary, extraordinary meetings of the permanent Council shall be convoked by its President at Geneva or elsewhere.

3. The President of the permanent Council shall be, for the duration of a year from February 9, 1934, date of the signature of the Balkan Entente Pact at Athens, the Minister of Foreign Affairs of Greece. February 9, 1935, the presidency of the per-

manent Council shall pass to the Minister of Foreign Affairs of Rumania, February 9, 1936 to the Minister of Foreign Affairs of Turkey, February 9, 1937 to the Minister of Foreign Affairs of Yugoslavia. The rotation shall continue in the future in the same manner, by alphabetical order : Greece, Rumania, Turkey, Yugoslavia, and for the duration of a year from February. The President shall take the initiative in fixing the date and place of meeting and the agenda and decisions to be taken.

4. In all questions which are discussed, as well as in all decisions which are taken, whether they concern the affairs of the States of the Balkan Entente alone, or whether they concern their relations with third parties, the principle of absolute equality of the four States of the Balkan Entente shall be rigorously respected.

5. An Economic Consultative Council of the States of the Balkan Entente for the progressive co-ordination of the economic interests of the four States, is constituted. It shall be composed of specialists and experts in economic, commercial and financial matters and shall function as an auxiliary organ of the permanent Council.

6. The permanent Council has the power to establish other temporary or permanent organs, commissions or committees either for special questions, or for groups of questions for study and for the preparation of solutions for the permanent Council. All of these organs shall have a consultative and auxiliary character.

7. A Secretariat for the permanent Council is created. Its seat shall always be for one year in the capital of the President of the permanent Council.[1]

---

[1] *Les Balkans,* October-November 1934, pp. 628-629.

APPENDIX V

STATUTE OF THE BALKAN ENTENTE ECONOMIC CONSULTATIVE COUNCIL

1. The Economic Council of the Balkan Entente is composed of four national sections : Greek, Rumanian, Turk, Yugoslav.

2. Each section shall have as members five delegates, namely :
   (a) For general commercial policy ;
   (b) For agricultural questions ;
   (c) For industrial questions ;
   (d) For financial questions, questions of credit and central banks ;
   (e) For communication questions.

3. In each section experts and specialists, having knowledge of practical economic life shall be nominated to assist the delegates in the examination of the economic activities of the four countries. The sections may also be divided into committees for the examination of special questions.

4. Each section will prepare its studies and its concrete propositions in its national meetings.
   The four sections shall meet regularly at least twice a year, in rotation in the capitals of the four States, to co-ordinate in their separate endeavours in the sections and to prepare their common propositions which shall be subsequently presented to the permanent Council for decision.

5. The detailed object of the studies of the economic council, as well as its rules of procedure will be the subject of a later decision by the permanent Council. For the time being, the permanent Council decides that in the coming five months the Economic Council shall meet once at Athens and once at Ankara in order to present, at the

next meeting of the Balkan Entente which will take place at Bucharest May 10, 1935, a temporary report on the following questions :

(a) Intensification of the economic and commercial relations between the States signatories of the Balkan Entente ;

(b) The development of inter-Balkan communications, especially those using the Danube and the Black Sea, which will permit increased exchanges of the Balkan States and Central Europe with Asia, as well as the other means of maritime communication ;

(c) The possibility of creating a Balkan Bank for foreigners ;

(d) Travel in general.[1]

[1] *Les Balkans, October-November* 1934, pp. 628-629.

APPENDIX VI

LITTLE ENTENTE PACT OF ORGANIZATION

SIGNED AT GENEVA 16TH FEBRUARY, 1933 ; RATIFICATIONS
EXCHANGED AT PRAGUE 30TH MAY, 1933

His Majesty the King of Yugoslavia,

His Majesty the King of Rumania,

His Excellency the President of the Czechoslovak Republic,

Being anxious to maintain and consolidate the peace ;

Being determined to strengthen economic relations without distinction with all States and with the Central European States in particular;

Being concerned for the safeguarding of peace in all circumstances, and to assure the evolution toward a real stabilization of conditions in Central Europe and to insure that the common interests of their three countries are respected ;

Determined for this purpose to give to the relations of friendship and alliance existing between the States of the Little Entente an organic and stable basis ;

Convinced of the necessity of realizing this stability on the one hand by the complete unification of their general policy and on the other by the creation of a directing organ of this policy common to the group of the three States of the Little Entente, and thus forming a higher international unity that shall be open to other States under conditions to be agreed upon in each particular case ;

Have resolved to establish what follows in the subjoined provisions :

Article 1

A Permanent Council of the States of the Little Entente, composed of the Ministers of Foreign Affairs of the three respective countries and of special delegates appointed for the purpose, shall be constituted as the directing organ of the common policy of the group of the three States. The decisions of the Permanent Council shall be unanimous.

Article 2

The Permanent Council, apart from its normal intercourse through diplomatic channels, shall assemble at least three times a year. One of the obligatory annual meetings shall take place in each of the three States in turn, and another shall be held at Geneva at the same time as the Assembly of the League of Nations.

Article 3

The President of the Permanent Council shall be the Minister of Foreign Affairs of the State in which the obligatory annual meeting is held. He shall take the initiative in fixing the date and the place of meeting, in arranging its agenda and in drawing up the questions to be decided. He shall continue to be President of the Permanent Council until the first obligatory meeting of the following year.

Article 4

In all questions which shall be discussed as well as in all decisions which shall be reached, whether in regard to the relations of the States of the Little Entente among themselves or in regard to the relations of the Little Entente with other States, the principle of the absolute equality of the three States of the Little Entente shall be rigorously respected.

Article 5

The Permanent Council shall determine whether, in a question upon which it has reached a decision, the presentation of the defence of the point of view of the States of the Little Entente shall be confided to a single delegate or to the delegation of a single State.

Article 6

Every political treaty of each State of the Little Entente and every unilateral act changing the present political situation of one of the States of the Little Entente in relation to an outside State, as well as every economic agreement involving important political consequences, shall henceforth require the unanimous consent of the Council of the Little Entente. The present political treaties of each State of the Little Entente with outside States shall be progressively and as far as possible unified.

Article 7

An Economic Council of the States of the Little Entente shall be constituted for the progressive co-ordination of the economic interests of the three States, whether among themselves or in their relations with other States.

Article 8

The Permanent Council shall be empowered to establish other stable temporary organs, commissions or committees for the purpose of studying and preparing the solution of special questions or groups of questions for the Permanent Council.

Article 9

A Secretariat of the Permanent Council shall be created. Its headquarters shall be established in turn for one year in the capital of the President for the time being of the Permanent Council. A section of the Secretariat shall function permanently at the headquarters of the League of Nations at Geneva.

Article 10

The common policy of the Permanent Council shall be inspired by the general principles contained in all the great international agreements relating to post-war policy, such as the Covenant of the League of Nations, the Pact of Paris, the General Act of Arbitration, the Locarno Pacts and the conventions that will eventually be made in regard to disarmament. Furthermore, nothing in the present Pact shall be construed as contrary to the principles or provisions of the Covenant of the League of Nations.

Article 11

The Conventions of Alliance between Rumania and Czechoslovakia of April 23, 1921, between Rumania and Yugoslavia of June 7, 1921, and between Czechoslovakia and Yugoslavia of August 31, 1922, whose terms were extended on May 21, 1929, and which are completed by the provisions of the present Pact, as well as the Act of Conciliation, Arbitration, and Judicial Settlement signed by the three States of the Little Entente at Belgrade on May 21, 1929, are hereby renewed for an indefinite period.

Article 12

The present Pact shall be ratified and the exchange of ratifications shall take place at Prague not later than at the next obligatory meeting. It shall come into effect on the day of the exchange of ratifications.

In witness whereof the plenipotentiaries named below have signed the present Pact.

Done at Geneva, in triplicate, the 16th day of February, 1933.

Jevtitch
Titulescu
Benes [1]

[1] *American Journal of International Law, Official Documents*, July 1933, pp. 117-119.

APPENDIX VII

ARGENTINE ANTI-WAR PACT

SIGNED AT RIO DE JANEIRO, 10TH OCTOBER, 1933

The states designated below, in the desire to contribute to the consolidation of peace, and to express their adherence to the efforts made by all civilized nations to promote the spirit of universal harmony ;

To the end of condemning wars of aggression and territorial acquisitions that may be obtained by armed conquest, making them impossible and establishing their invalidity through the positive provisions of this treaty, and in order to replace them with pacific solutions based on lofty concepts of justice and equity ;

Convinced that one of the most effective means of assuring the moral and material benefits which peace offers to the world, is the organization of a permanent system of conciliation for international disputes, to be applied immediately on the violation of the principles mentioned :

Have decided to put these aims of non-aggression and concord in conventional form, by concluding the present treaty, to which end they have appointed the undersigned plenipotentiaries, who, having exhibited their respective full powers, found to be in good and due form, have agreed upon the following:

Article 1

The high contracting parties solemnly declare that they condemn wars of aggression in their mutual relations or those with other states, and that the settlement of disputes or controversies of any kind that may arise among them shall be effected only by the pacific means which have the sanction of international law.

Article 2

They declare that as between the high contracting parties, territorial questions must not be settled by violence, and that they will not recognize any territorial arrangement which is not obtained by pacific means, nor the validity of the occupation or acquisition of territories that may be brought about by force of arms.

Article 3

In case of noncompliance by any state engaged in a dispute, with the obligations contained in the foregoing articles, the contracting states undertake to make every effort for the maintenance of peace. To that end they will adopt in their character as neutrals a common and solidary attitude ; they will exercise the political, juridical or economic means authorized by international law ; they will bring the influence of public opinion to bear but will in no case resort to intervention either diplomatic or armed ; subject to the attitude that may be incumbent on them by virtue of other collective treaties to which such states are signatories.

Article 4

The high contracting parties obligate themselves to submit to the conciliation procedure established by this treaty, the disputes specially mentioned and any others that may arise in their reciprocal relations, without further limitations than those enumerated in the following article, in all controversies which it has not been possible to settle by diplomatic means within a reasonable period of time.

Article 5

The high contracting parties and the states which may in the future adhere to this treaty, may not formulate at the time of signature, ratification or adherence, other limitations to the conciliation procedure than those which are indicated below :

(a) Differences for the solution of which treaties, conventions, pacts or pacific agreements of any kind whatever may have been concluded, which in no case shall be considered as annulled by this agreement, but supplemented thereby in so far as they tend to assure peace ; as well as the questions or matters settled by previous treaties ;

(b) Disputes which the parties prefer to solve by direct settlement or submit by common agreement to an arbitral or judicial solution ;

(c) Questions which international law leaves to the exclusive competence of each state, under its constitutional system, for which reason the parties may object to their being submitted to the conciliation procedure before the national or local jurisdiction has decided definitively ; except in the case of manifest denial or delay of justice, in which case the conciliation procedure shall be initiated within a year at the latest ;

(d) Matters which affect constitutional precepts of the parties to the controversy. In case of doubt, each party shall obtain the reasoned opinion of its respective tribunal or supreme court of justice, if the latter should be invested with such powers.

The high contracting parties may communicate, at any time and in the manner provided for by Article 15, an instrument stating that they have abandoned wholly or in part the limitations established by them in the conciliation procedure.

The effect of the limitations formulated by one of the contracting parties shall be that the other parties shall not consider themselves obligated in regard to that party save in the measure of the exceptions established.

Article 6

In the absence of a permanent conciliation commission or some other international organization charged with this mission by virtue of previous treaties in effect, the high contracting parties undertake to submit their differences to the examination and investigation of a Conciliation Commission which shall be formed as follows, unless there is an agreement to the contrary of the parties in each case :

The Conciliation Commission shall consist of five members. Each party to the controversy shall designate a member who may be chosen by it from among its own nationals. The three remaining members shall be designated by common agreement by the parties from among the nationals of third Powers, who must be of different nationalities, must not have their customary residence in the territory of the interested parties nor be in the service of any of them. The parties shall choose the president of the Conciliation Commission from among the said three members.

If they cannot arrive at an agreement with regard to such designations, they may entrust the selection thereof to a third Power or to some other existing international organism. If the candidates so designated are rejected by the parties or by any one of them, each party shall present a list of candidates equal in number to that of the members to be selected, and the names of those to sit on the Conciliation Commission shall be determined by lot.

Article 7

The tribunals or supreme courts of justice which, in accordance with the domestic legislation of each state, may be competent to interpret, in the last or the sole instance and in matters under their respective jurisdiction, the Constitution, treaties, or the general principles of the law of nations, may be designated preferentially by the high contracting parties to discharge the duties entrusted by the present treaty to the Conciliation Commission. In this case the tribunal or court may be constituted by the whole bench or may designate some of its members to proceed alone or by forming a mixed commission with members of other courts or tribunals, as may be agreed upon by common accord between the parties to the dispute.

Article 8

The Conciliation Commission shall establish its own rules of procedure, which shall provide in all cases for hearing both sides.

The parties to the controversy may furnish and the commission may require from them all the antecedents and information necessary. The parties may have themselves represented by delegates and assisted by advisers or experts, and also present evidence of all kinds.

Article 9

The labors and deliberations of the Conciliation Commission shall not be made public except by a decision of its own to that effect, with the assent of the parties.

In the absence of any stipulations to the contrary, the decisions of the commission shall be made by a majority vote, but the commission may not pronounce judgment on the substance of the case except in the presence of all its members.

Article 10

It is the duty of the commission to secure the conciliatory settlement of the disputes submitted to its consideration.

After an impartial study of the questions in dispute, it shall set forth in a report the outcome of its work and shall propose to the parties bases of settlement by means of a just and equitable solution.

The report of the commission shall in no case have the character of a final decision or arbitral award either with respect to the exposition or the interpretation of the facts, or with regard to the considerations or conclusions of law.

Article 11

The Conciliation Commission must present its report within one year counting from its first meeting unless the parties should decide by common agreement to shorten or extend this period.

The conciliation procedure having been once begun may be interrupted only by a direct settlement between the parties or by their subsequent decision to submit the dispute by common accord to arbitration or to international justice.

Article 12

In communicating its report to the parties, the Conciliation Commission shall fix for them a period which shall not exceed six months, within which they must decide as to the bases of the settlement it has proposed. On the expiration of this term, the commission shall record in a final act the decision of the parties.

This period having expired without acceptance of the settlement by the parties, or the adoption by common accord of another friendly solution, the parties to the dispute shall regain their freedom of action to proceed as they may see fit within the limitations flowing from Articles 1 and 2 of this treaty.

Article 13

From the initiation of the conciliatory procedure until the expiration of the period fixed by the commission for the parties to make a decision, they must abstain from any measure prejudicial to the execution of the agreement that may be proposed by the commission and, in general, from any act capable of aggravating or prolonging the controversy.

Article 14

During the conciliation procedure the members of the commission shall receive honoraria the amount of which shall be established by common agreement by the parties to the controversy. Each of them shall bear its own expenses, and a moiety of the joint expenses or honoraria.

Article 15

The present treaty shall be ratified by the high contracting parties as soon as possible, in accordance with their respective constitutional procedures.

The original treaty and the instruments of ratification shall be deposited in the Ministry of Foreign Relations, of the Argentine Republic, which shall communicate the ratifications to the other signatory states. The treaty shall go into effect between the high contracting parties thirty days after the deposit of the respective ratifications, and in the order in which they are effected.

Article 16

This treaty shall remain open to the adherence of all states.

Adherence shall be effected by the deposit of the respective instrument in the Ministry of Foreign Relations of the Argentine Republic, which shall give notice thereof to the other interested states.

Article 17

The present treaty is concluded for an indefinite time, but may be denounced by one year's notice, on the expiration of which the effects thereof shall cease for the denouncing state, and remain in force for the other states which are parties thereto, by signature or adherence.

The denunciation shall be addressed to the Ministry of Foreign Relations of the Argentine Republic, which shall transmit it to the other interested states.

In witness whereof . . . [1]

[1] *Press Release*, Dept. of State, 28th April, 1934 ; *American Journal of International Law, Official Documents*, July 1934, p. 79 et seq.

INDEX

A

Adriatic Sea, 19.

Ægean Sea, 6, 19, 75, 76, 99, 114, 125.

Aërial communications, 48, 62, 80, 88, 133.

Aëronautical Office, Balkan, 88.

Agenda
First Balkan Conference, 10.
Second Balkan Conference, 24-25, 29.
Third Balkan Conference, 38, 48-49.
Fourth Balkan Conference, 70, 79-80, 83.
Fifth Balkan Conference, 102.

Aggression defined, 74, 82, 105, 106, 107, 136.
London Conventions Defining, 74-75, 83, 105-107.

Agrarian co-operation and conferences, 25, 26, 66, 72.
Effect upon Balkan movement, 26-27, 66.

Agriculture
Balkan Chamber of, 32, 48, 59-60, 79.
Agricultural banks, 86.
Agricultural credit, 48, 59, 60, 79, 86.

Albania
and Balkan Conferences, 11, 24, 28, 30, 42, 46, 47, 50, 80-81, 109.
and Balkan Entente, 28, 91, 115, 118, 135.
relations with Bulgaria, 7, 42, 103, 104, 137.
Greece, 7, 50, 80-81, 88, 101, 103, 109, 137, 146.
Italy, 91, 103-104, 137, 143.
Rumania, 50.
Turkey, 7, 80-81, 137.

Yugoslavia, 7, 88, 90, 98, 103-104, 137.

Alexander, King of Yugoslavia, 77, 98, 112-116, 134.

Aliens, 48, 63.

Amphyctionic Councils, 21.

Ankara, 34, 77, 115, 123, 132.

Arbitration, 27, 30, 31, 41, 52-54, 58, 117, 122.
Hague Convention of. See Hague.

Argentine Anti-War Pact, 84, 116-122, 137, 145, Appendix VII.

Armed bands, 101.

Armed Neutralities, 121.

Athens, 9, 11, 19, 25, 33, 38, 39, 40, 62, 72, 91, 101, 115.

Austria-Hungary, 2, 4.
Recreation of old empire, 66, 67.

B

Balance of power, 73.

Balkan Conferences
First Conference, 11-22.
Second Conference, 28-35.
Third Conference, 45-65.
Fourth Conference, 78-89.
Fifth Conference, 109-112.
Adjourned *sine die*, 109-112.
Bureau of, 13, 15.
Commissions of
See Economic, Communications, Intellectual, Organization, Political, Social.
Conversion to semi-official group, 111-112.
Council of, 13, 15, 23-25, 31, 35-38, 44-45, 49, 50, 59, 60, 61, 64, 68, 69-72, 78, 83, 108-112.
Draft Pact, 31, 36, 44, 46, 48, 51, 52-59, 63, 64, 70, 76,